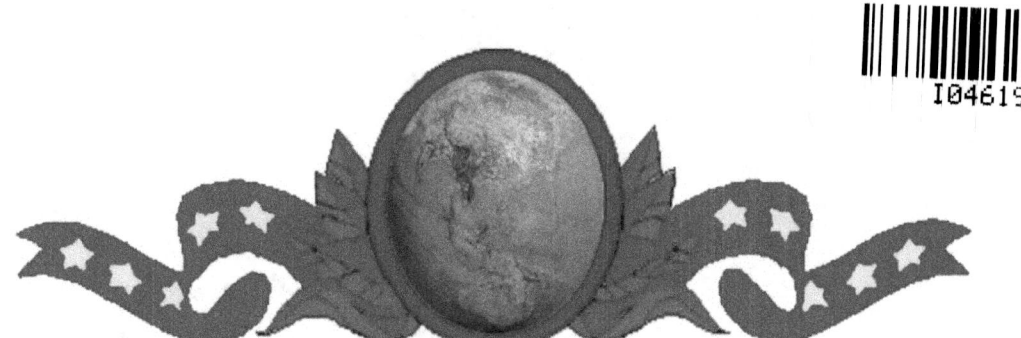

Real World

Colouring Book

For Advanced Users & Adults

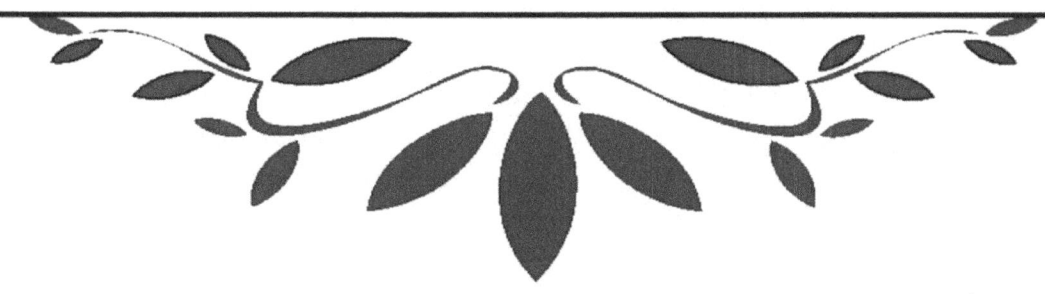

Copyright 2019 By John Boom

50 Images

Created From Real Life Photos
For You To Colour As You Please.

ISBN 978-0-359-78845-3

9 780359 788453

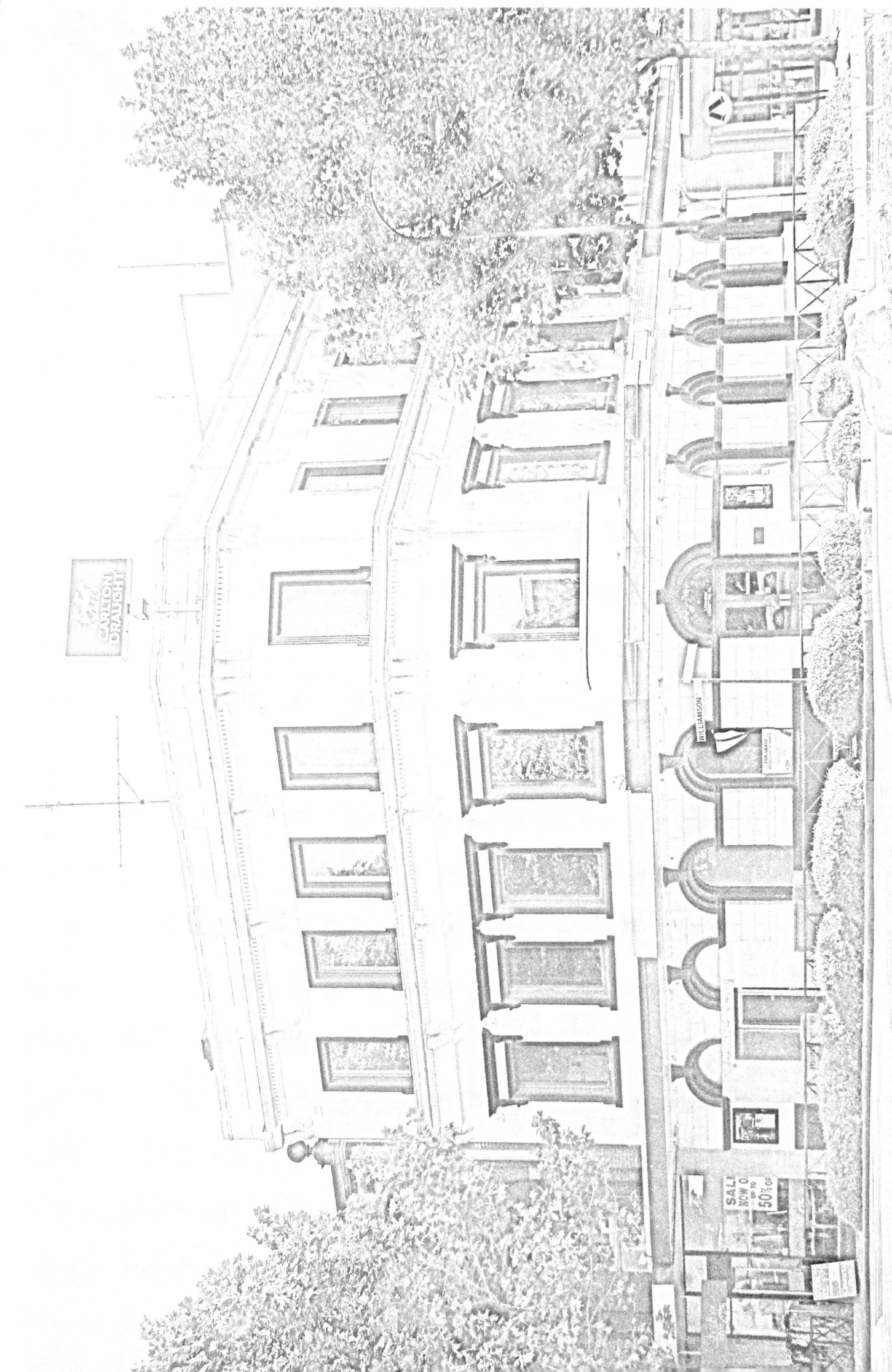

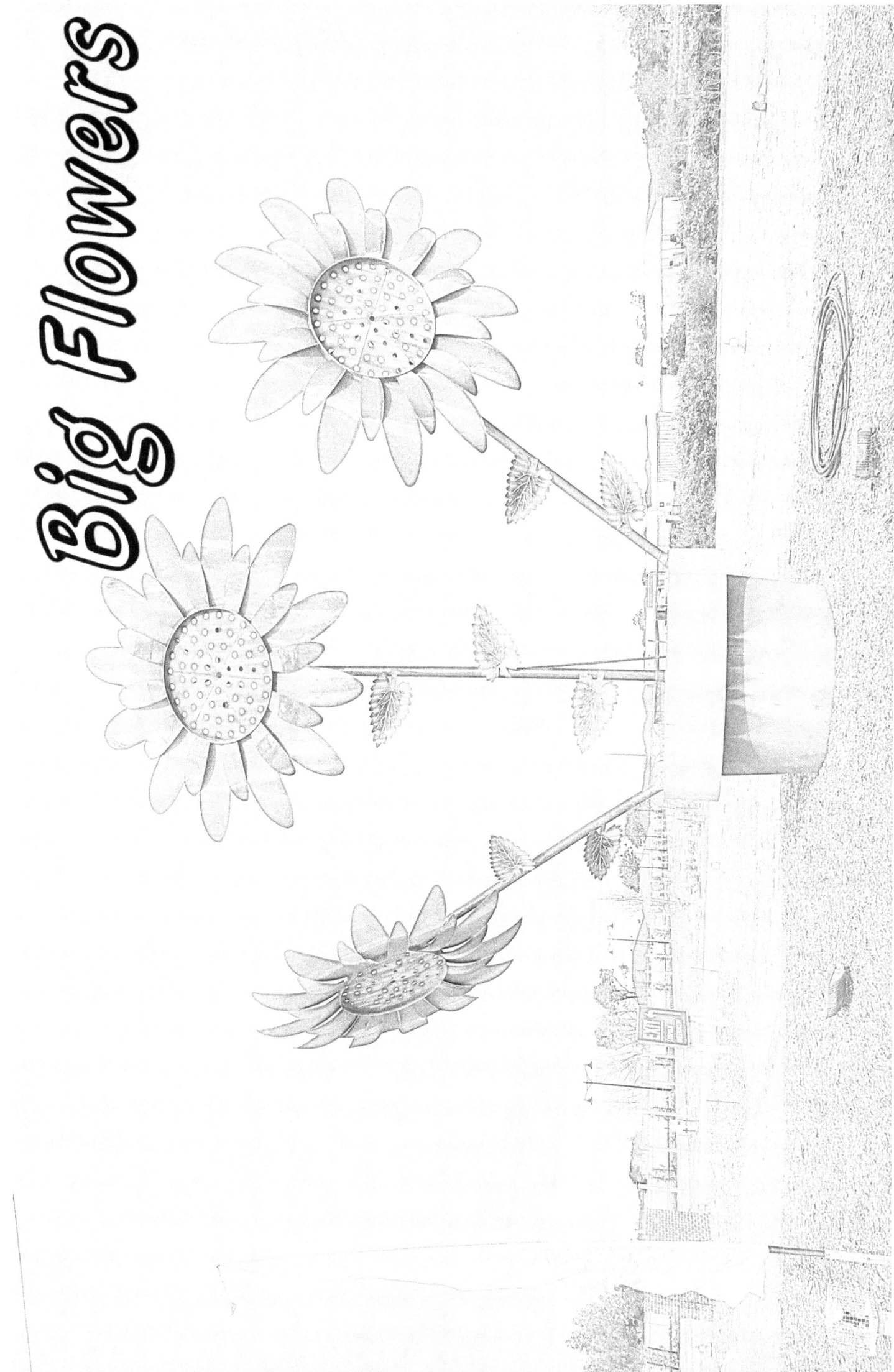

Big Flowers

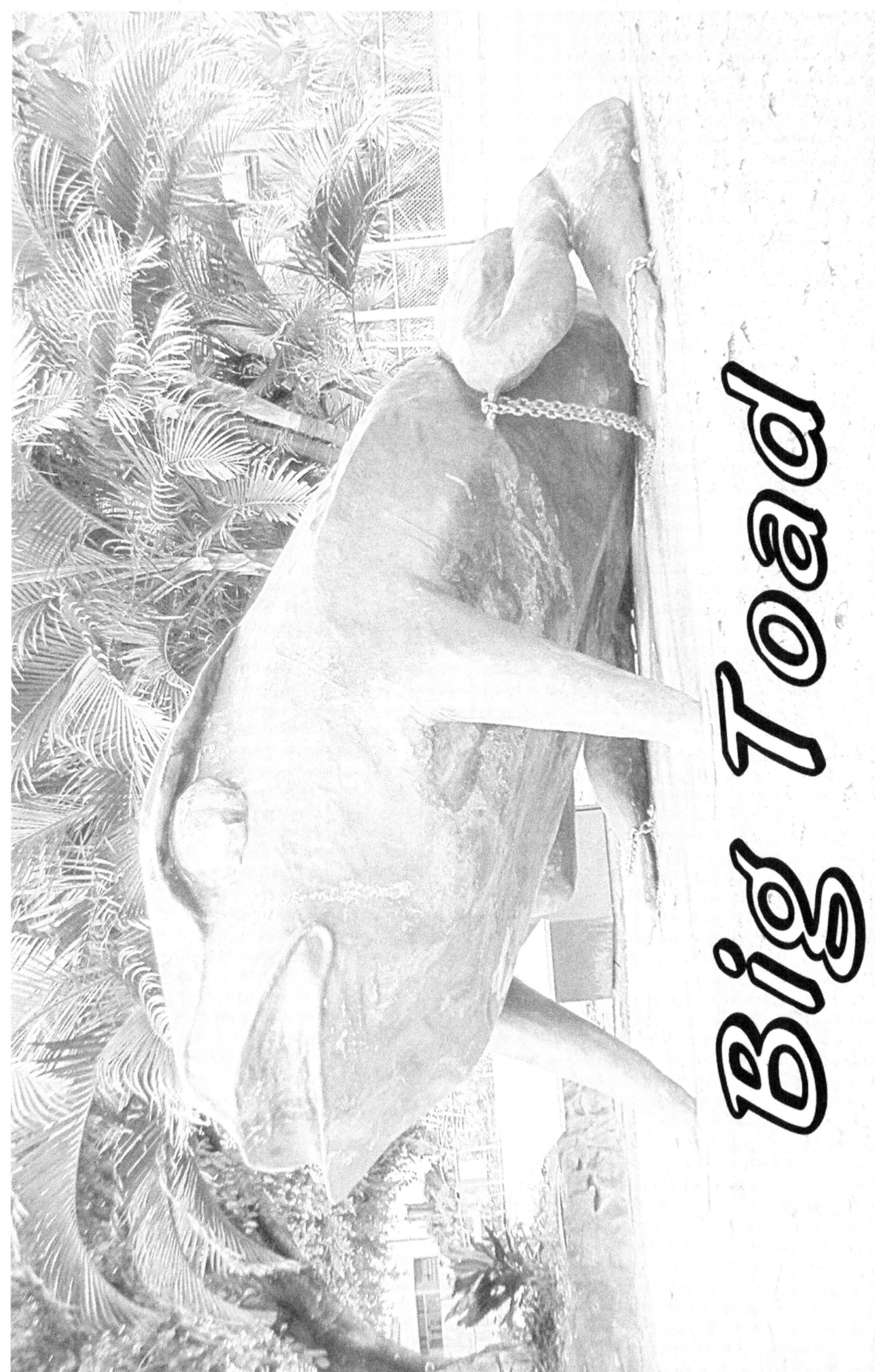

Big Toad

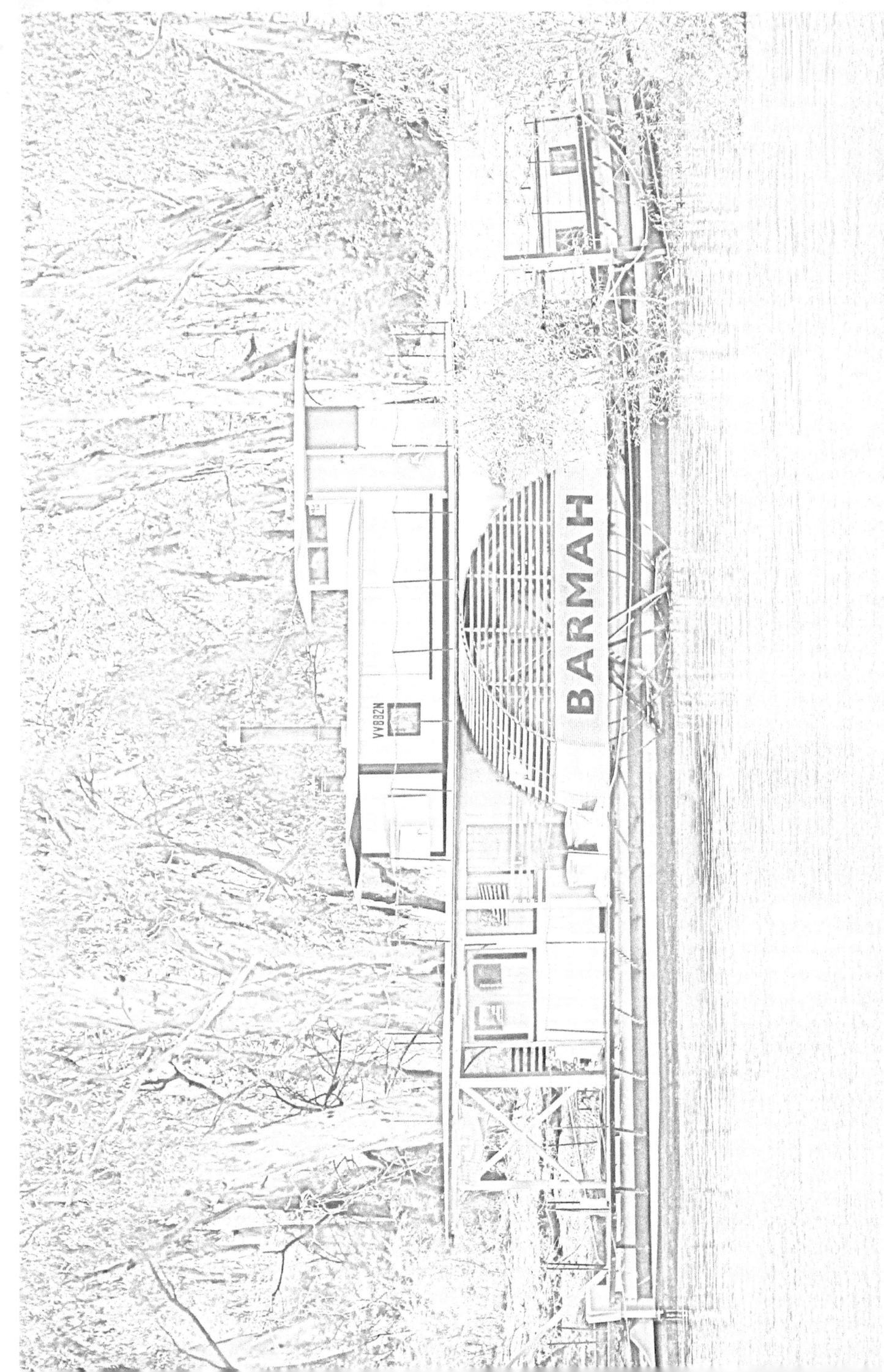

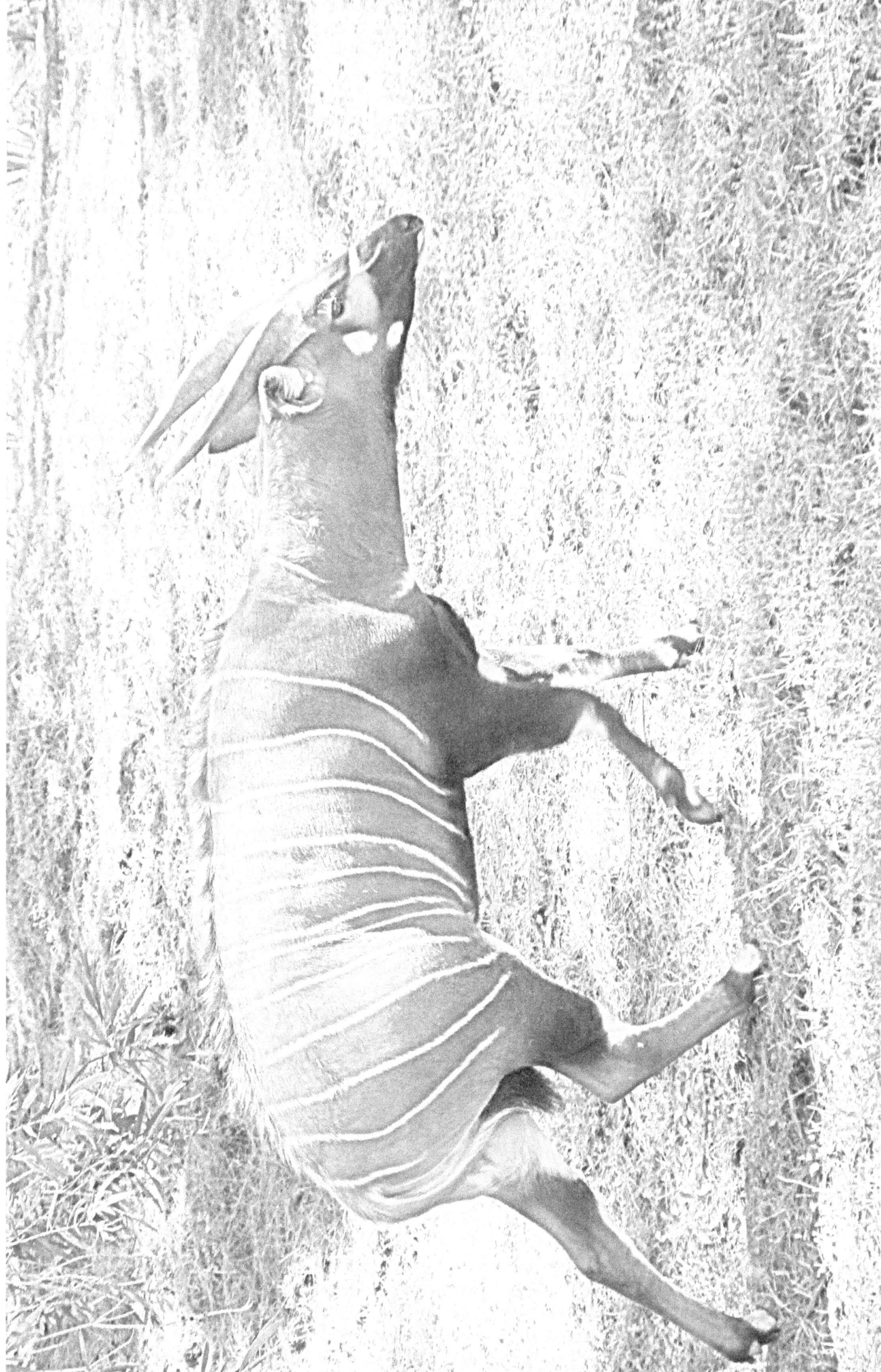

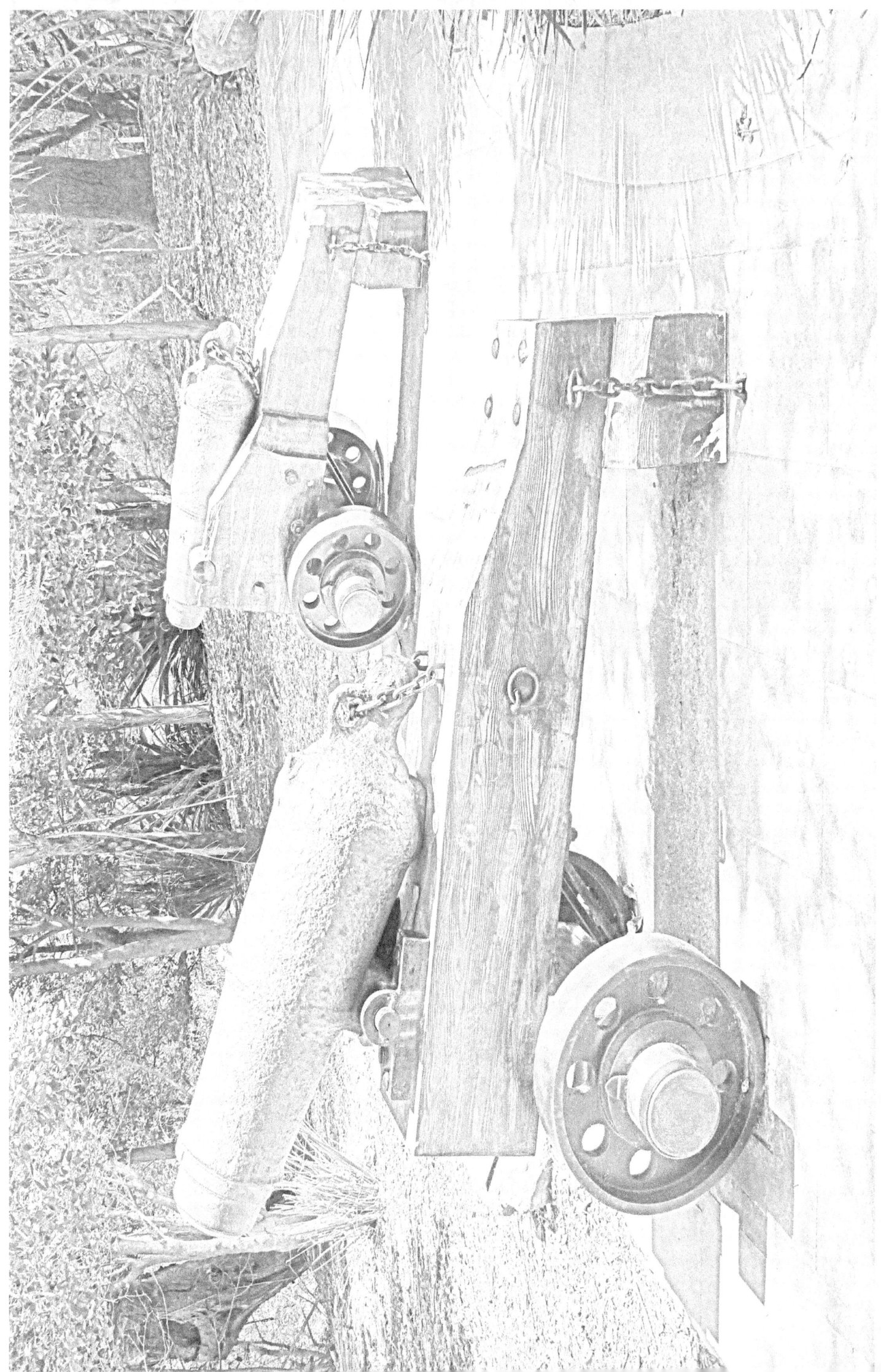

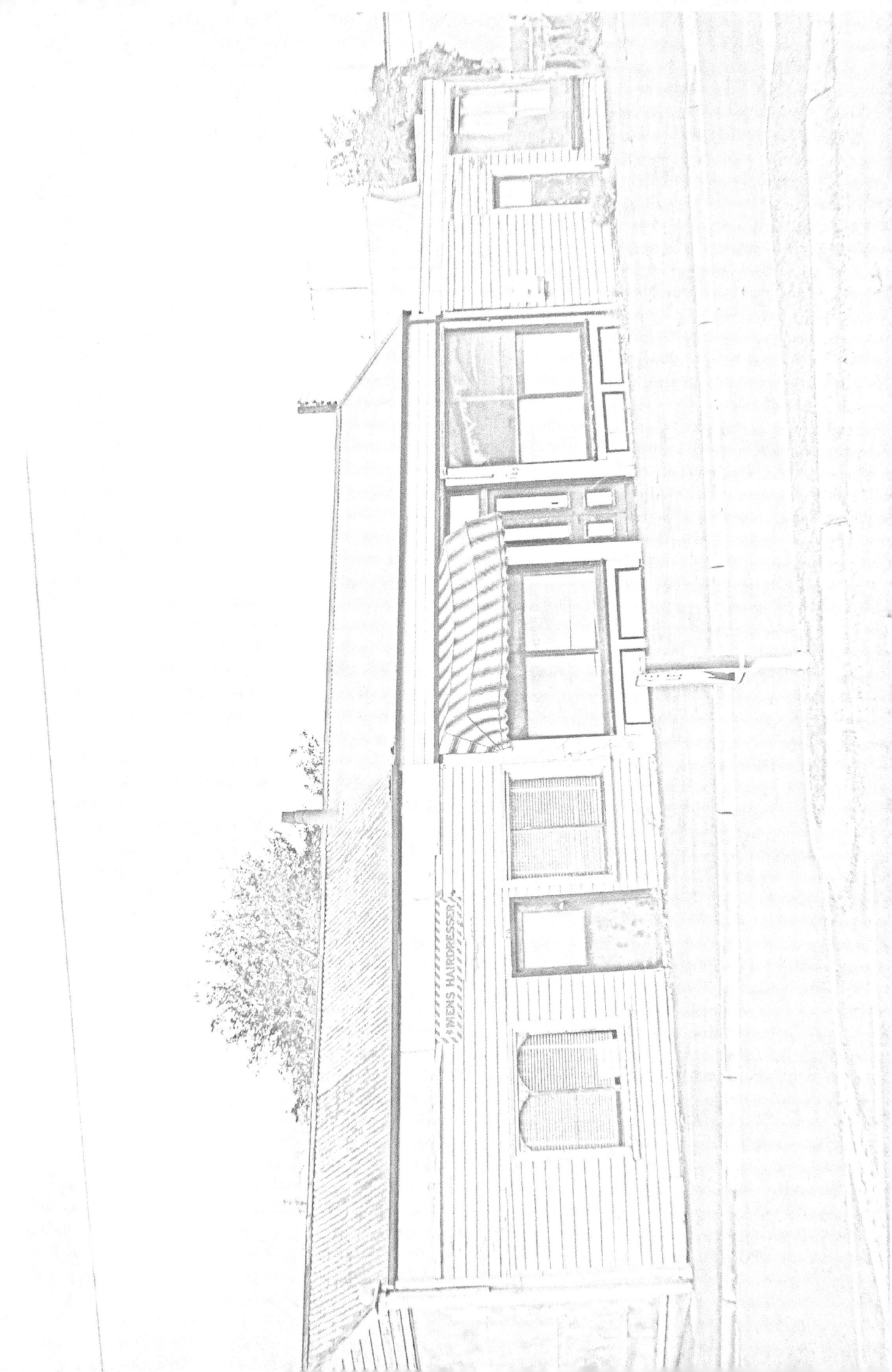

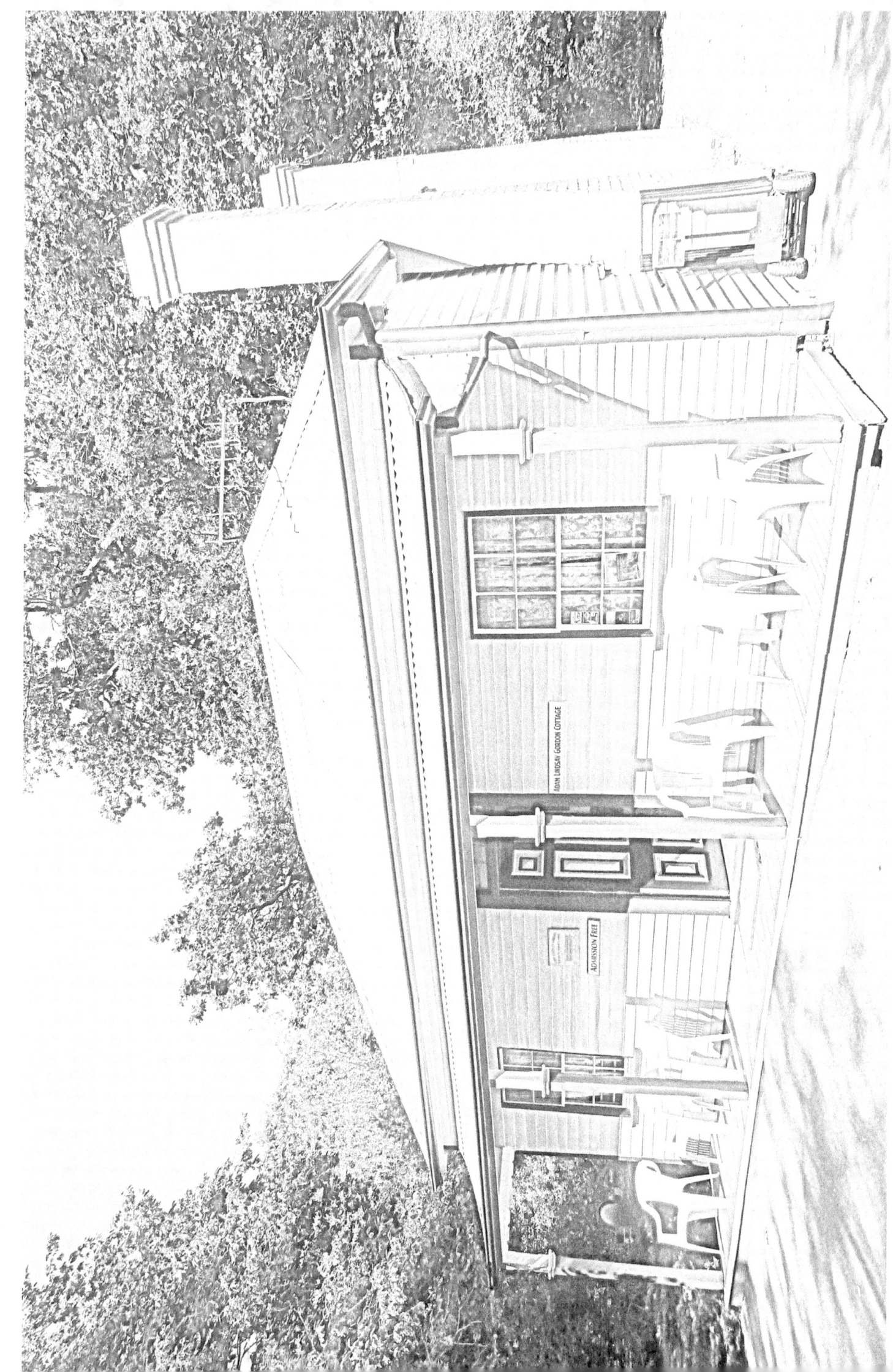

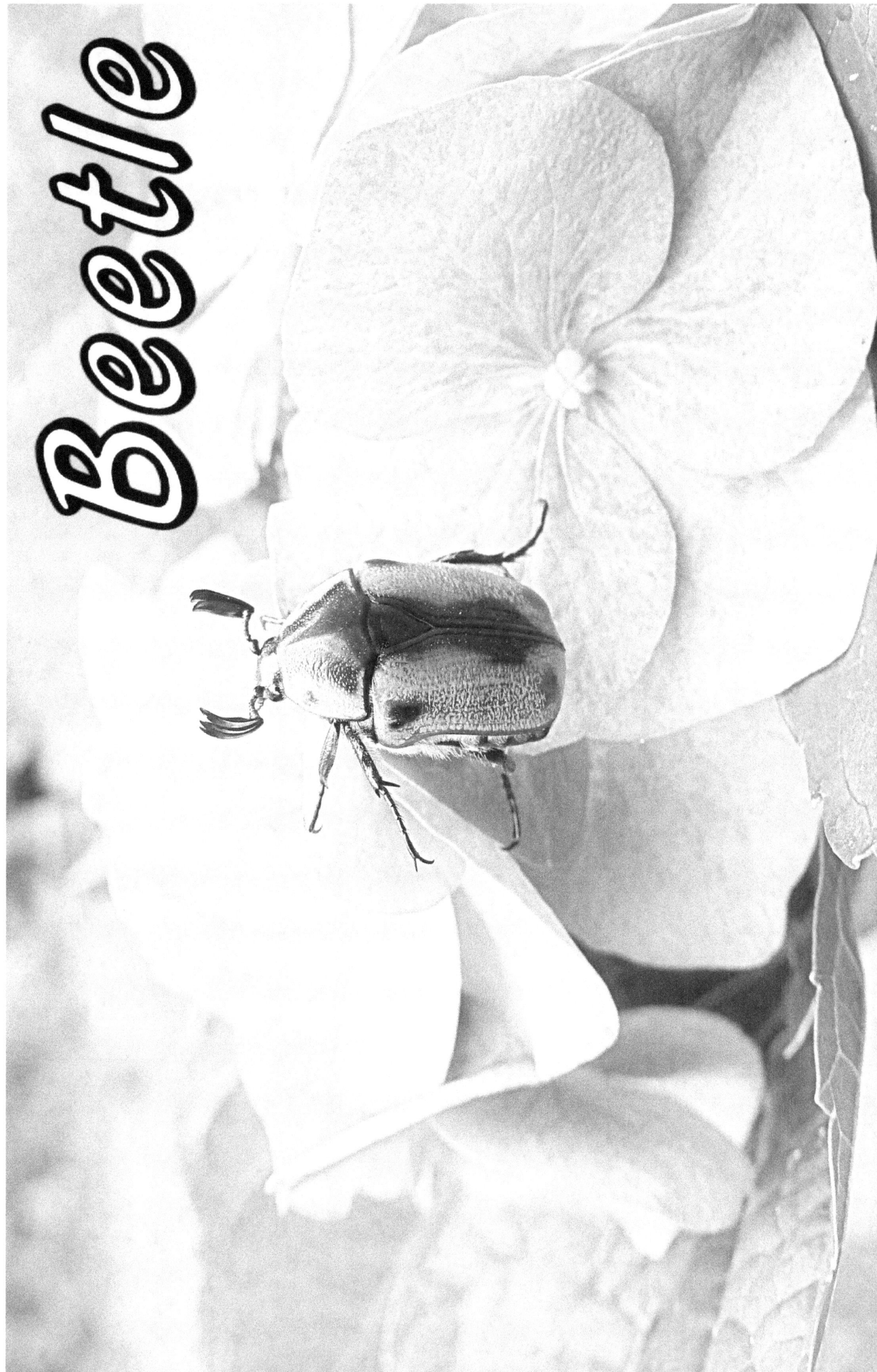

Beeetle

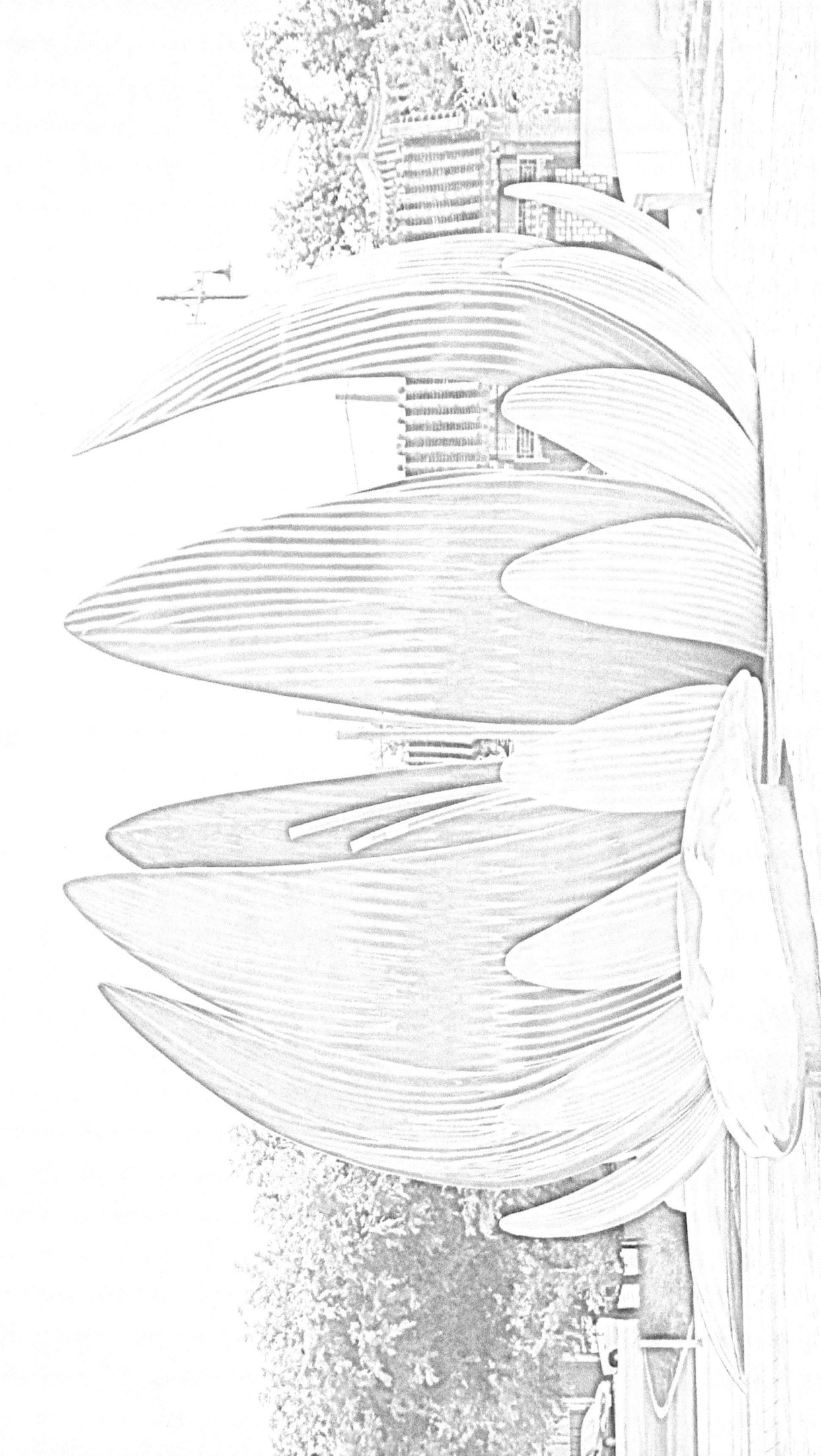

Big Fossil

KRONOSAURUS KORNER
Regional Visitor Information Centre
MARINE FOSSIL DISPLAY SOUVENIRS MAPS
Home Rock Cafe   Public Toilets
Australia's Best Vertebrate Fossils

MOTEL

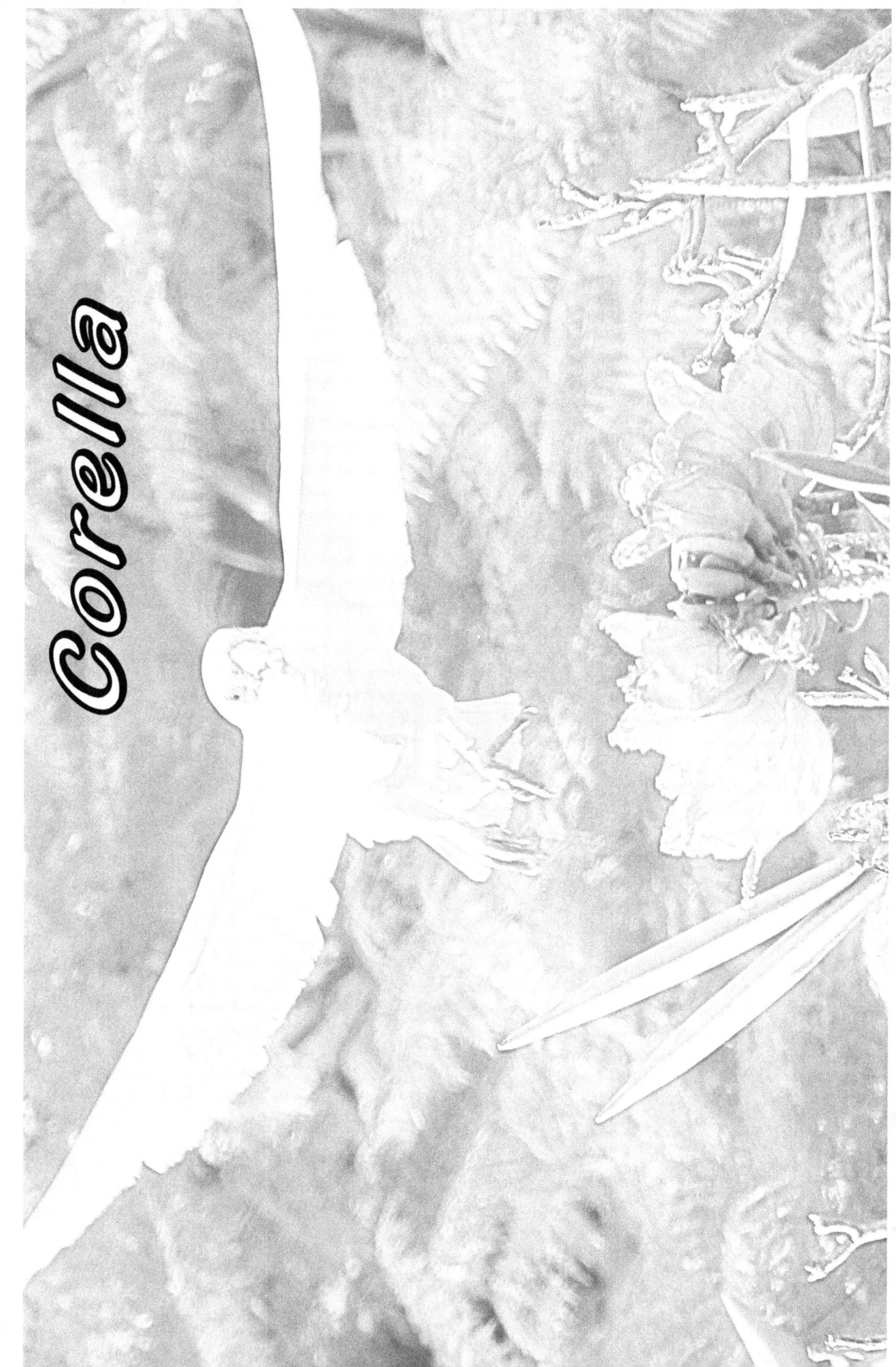

Corella

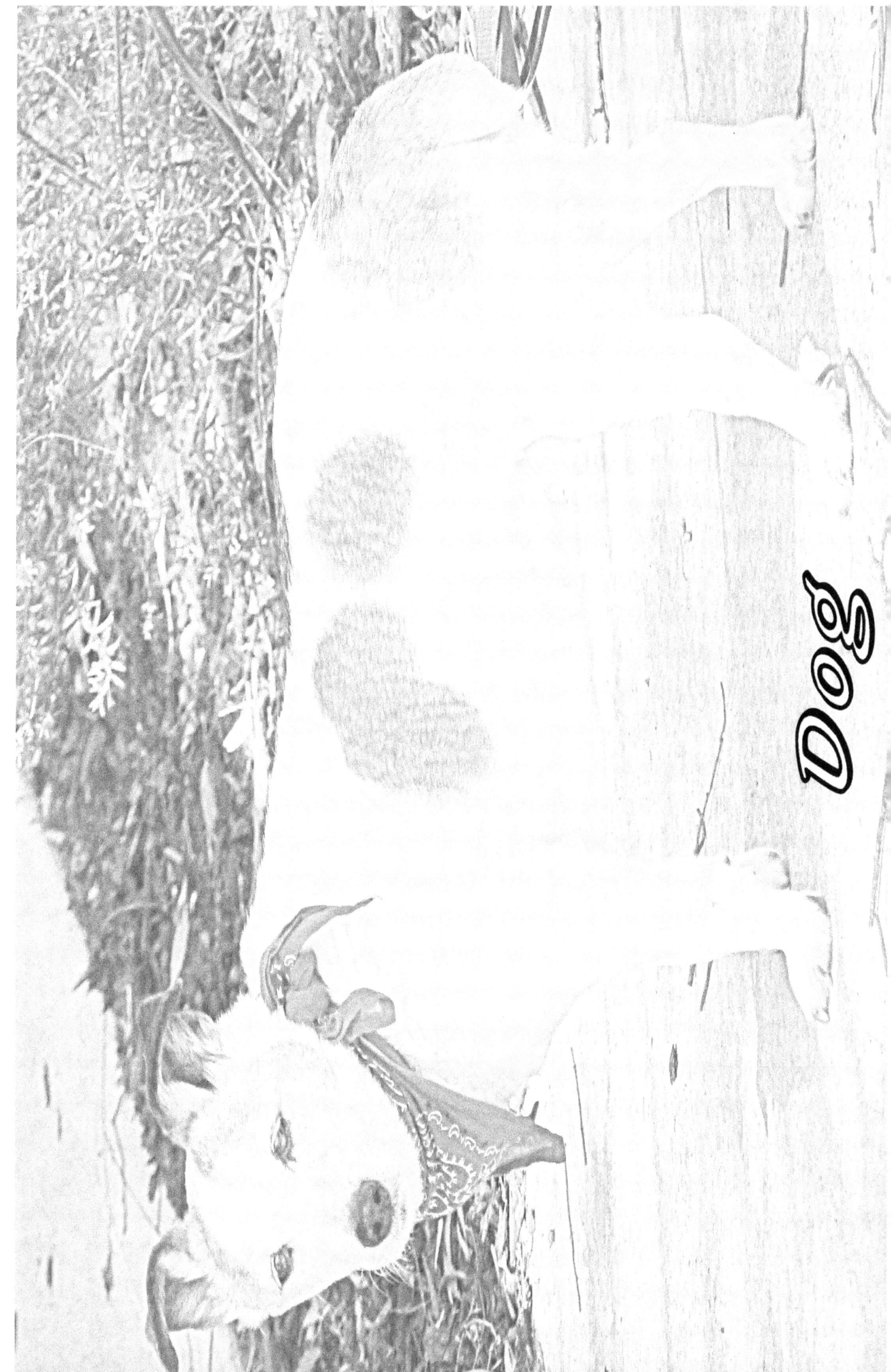

Dog

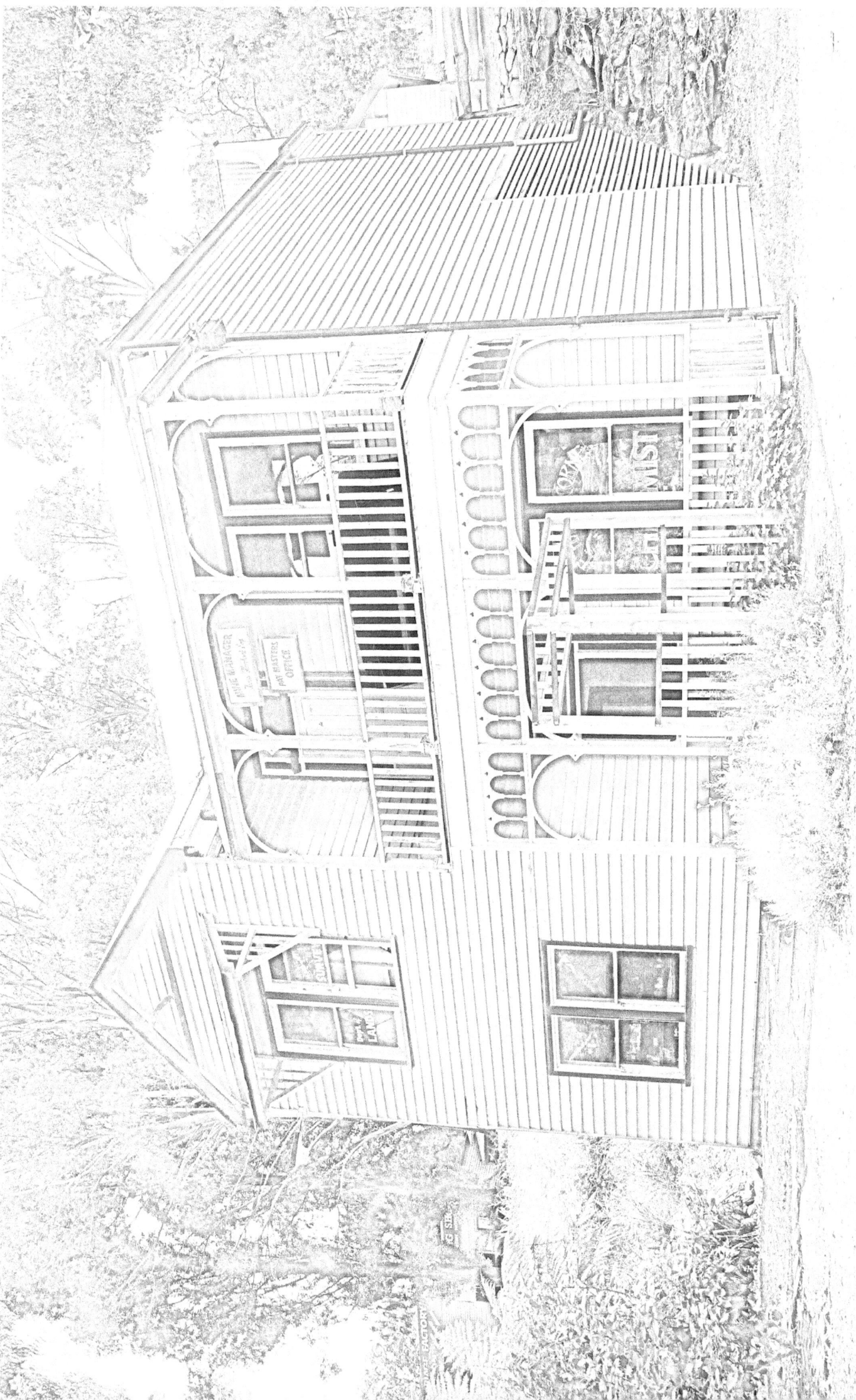

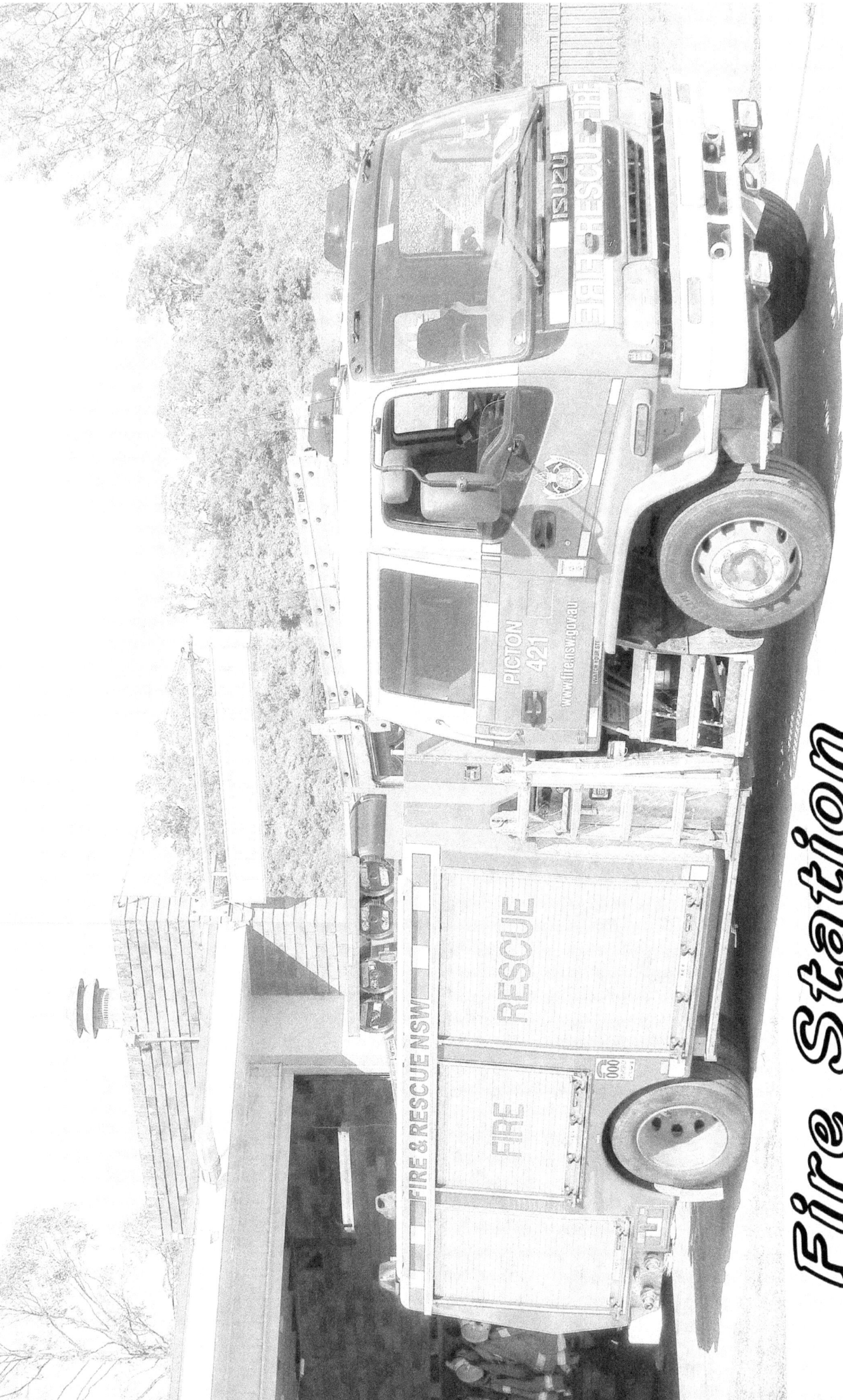

Fire Station

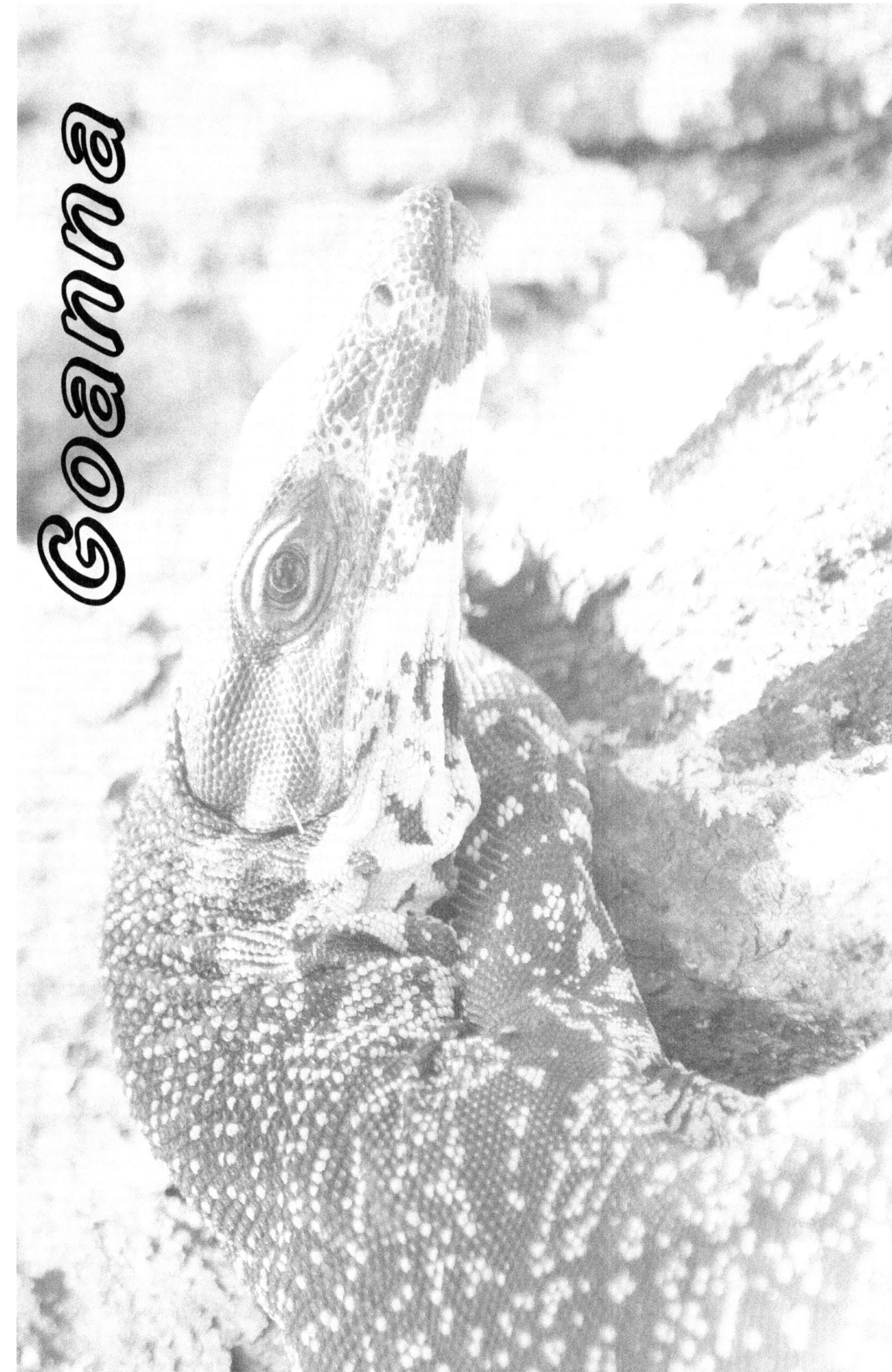

Goanna

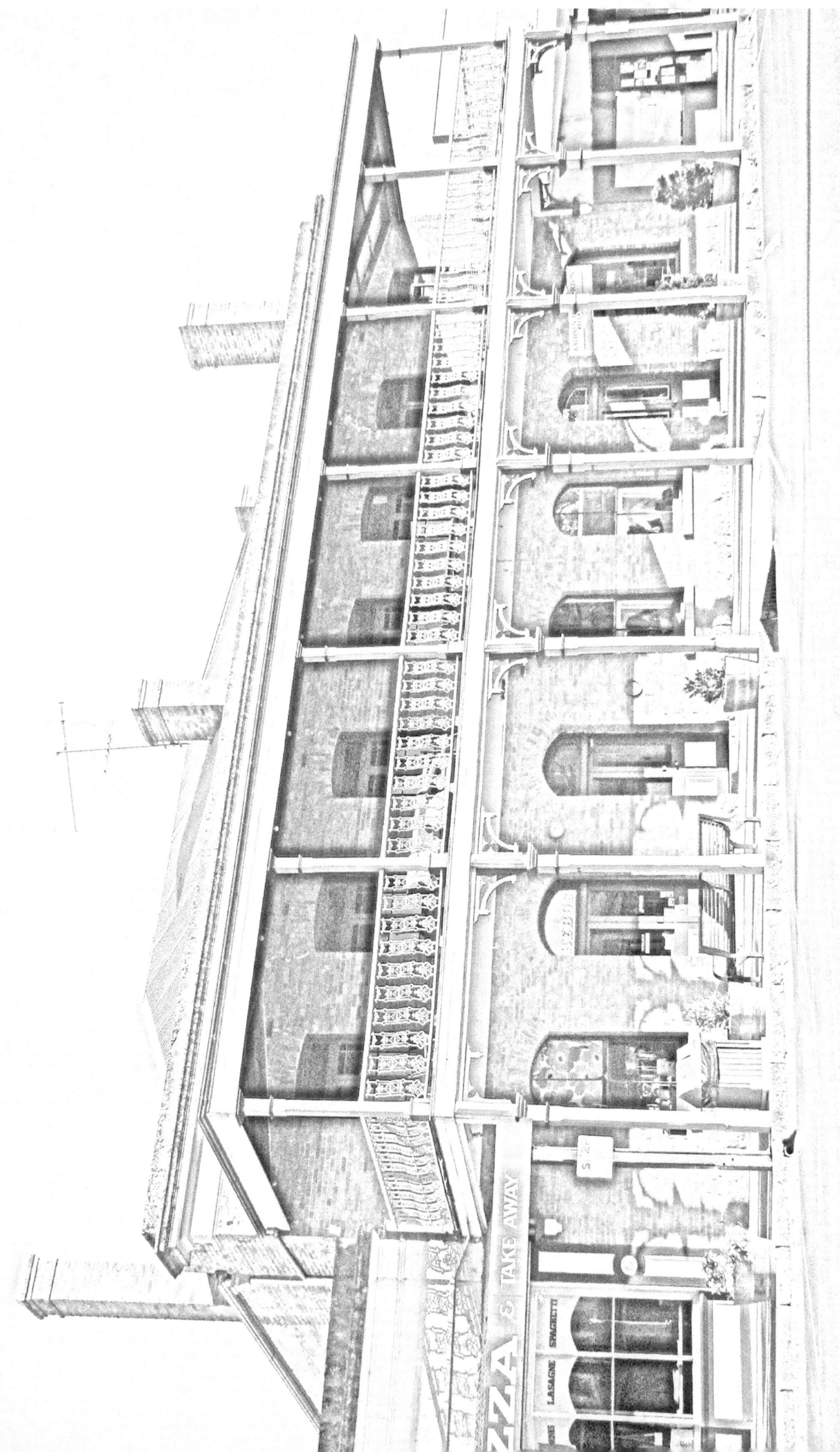

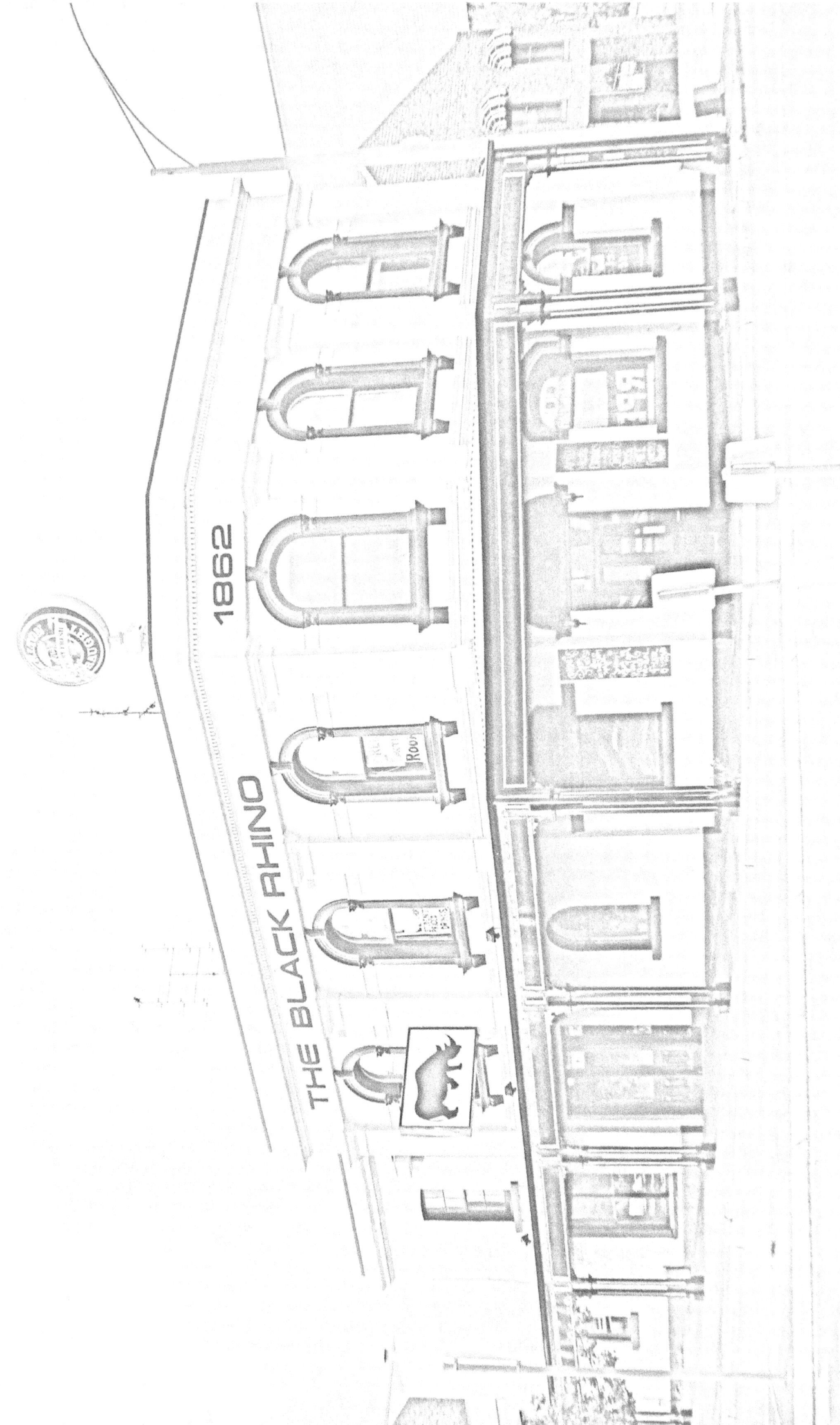

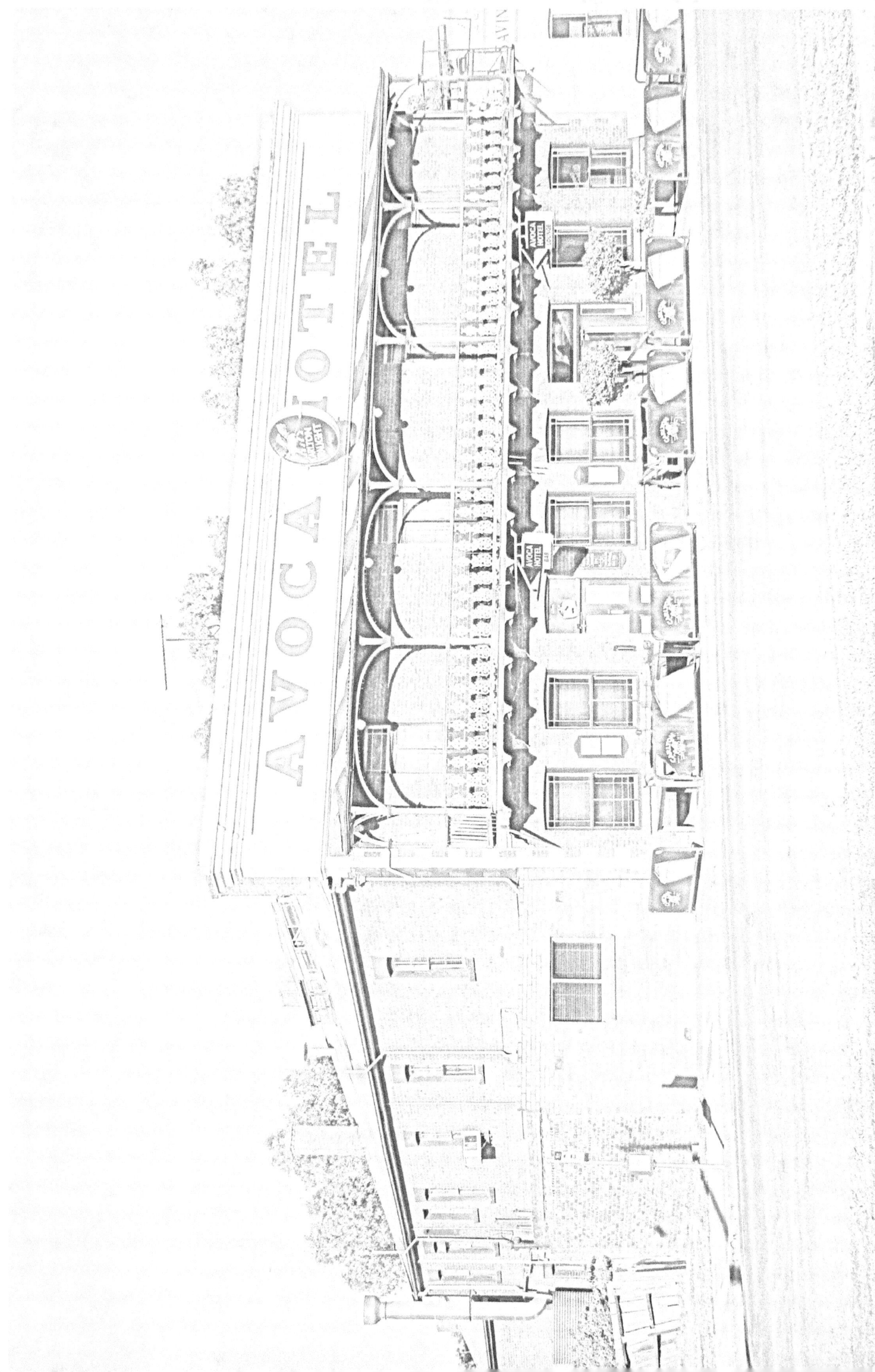

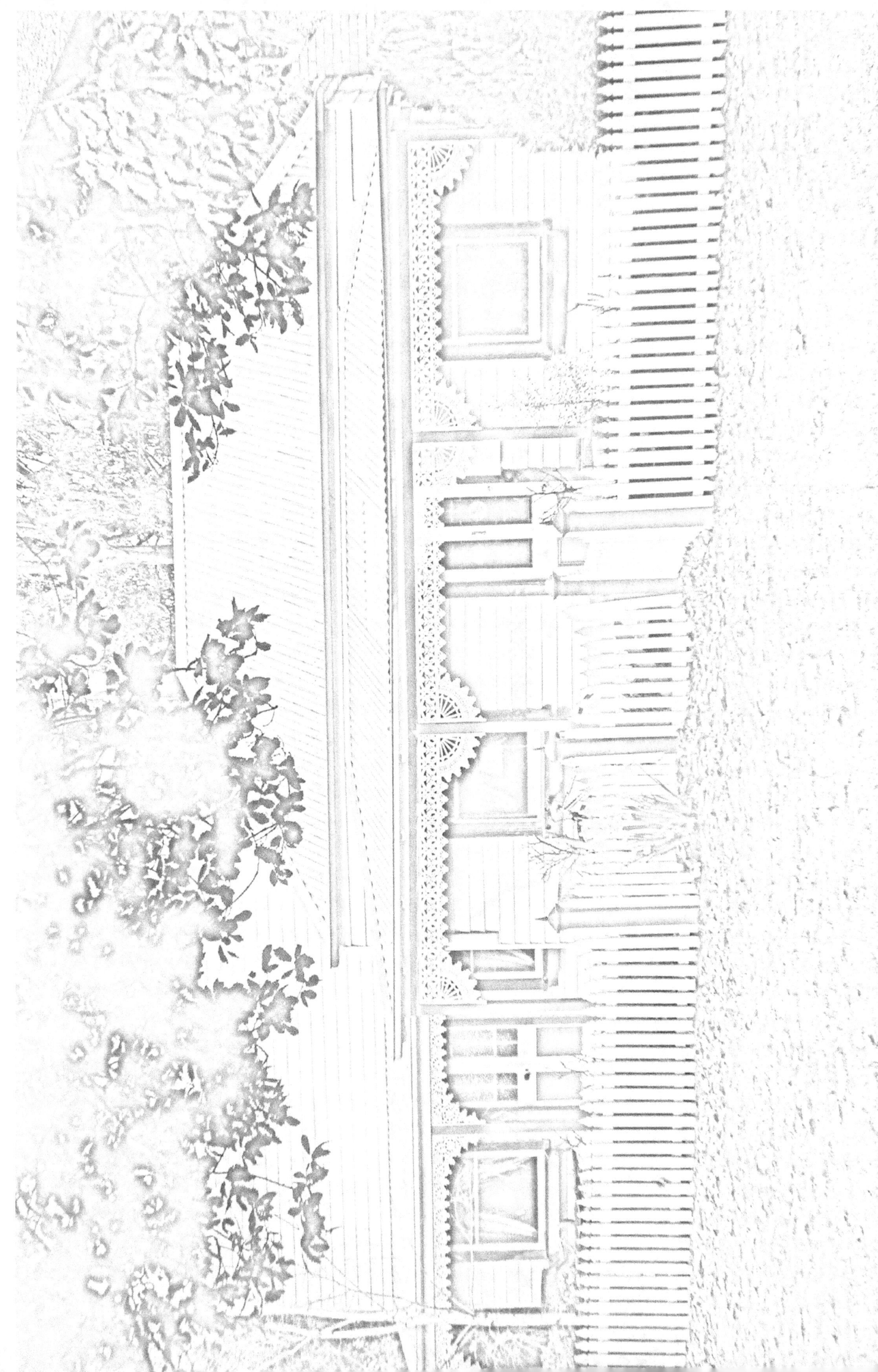

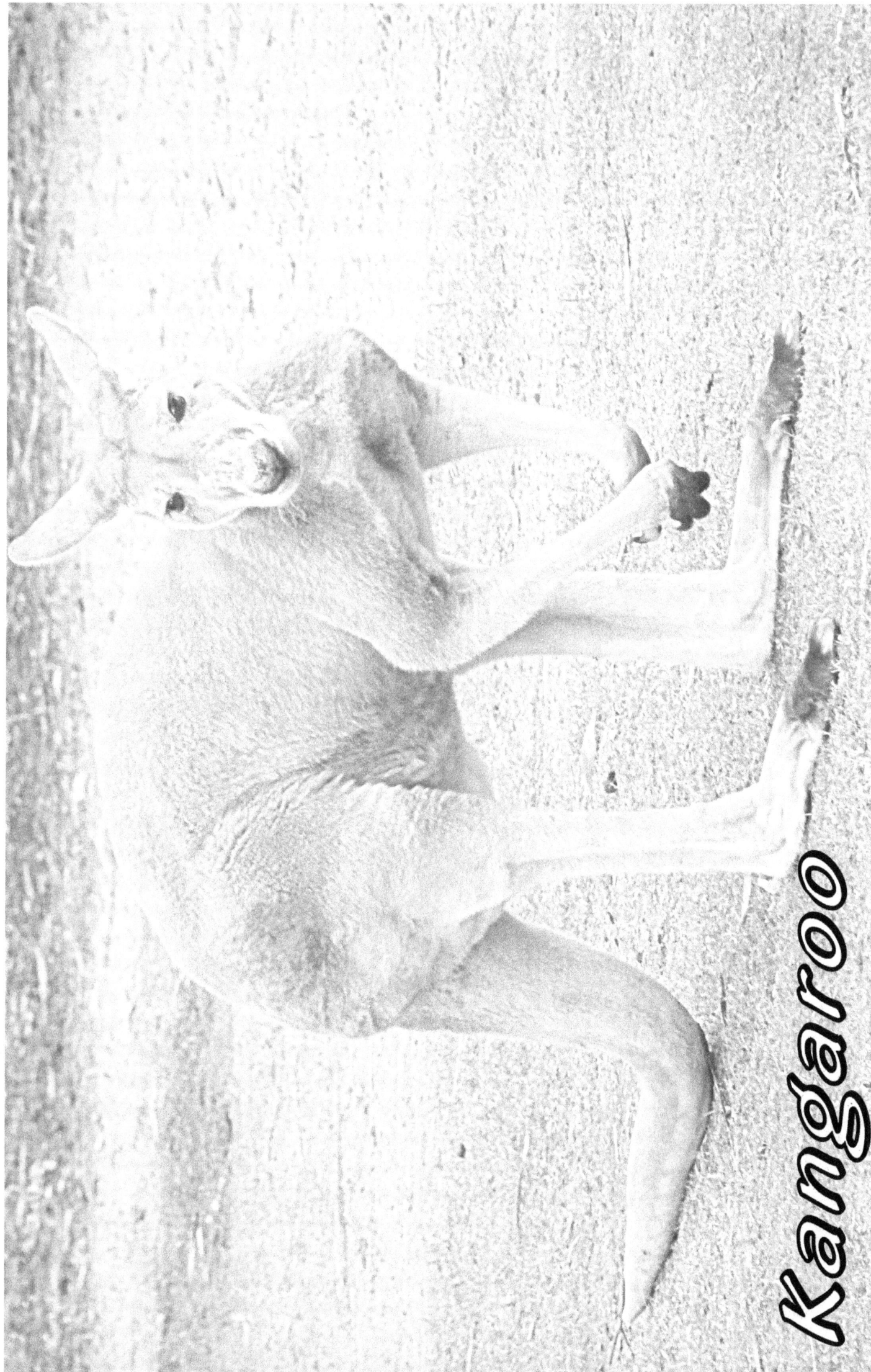

Kangaroo

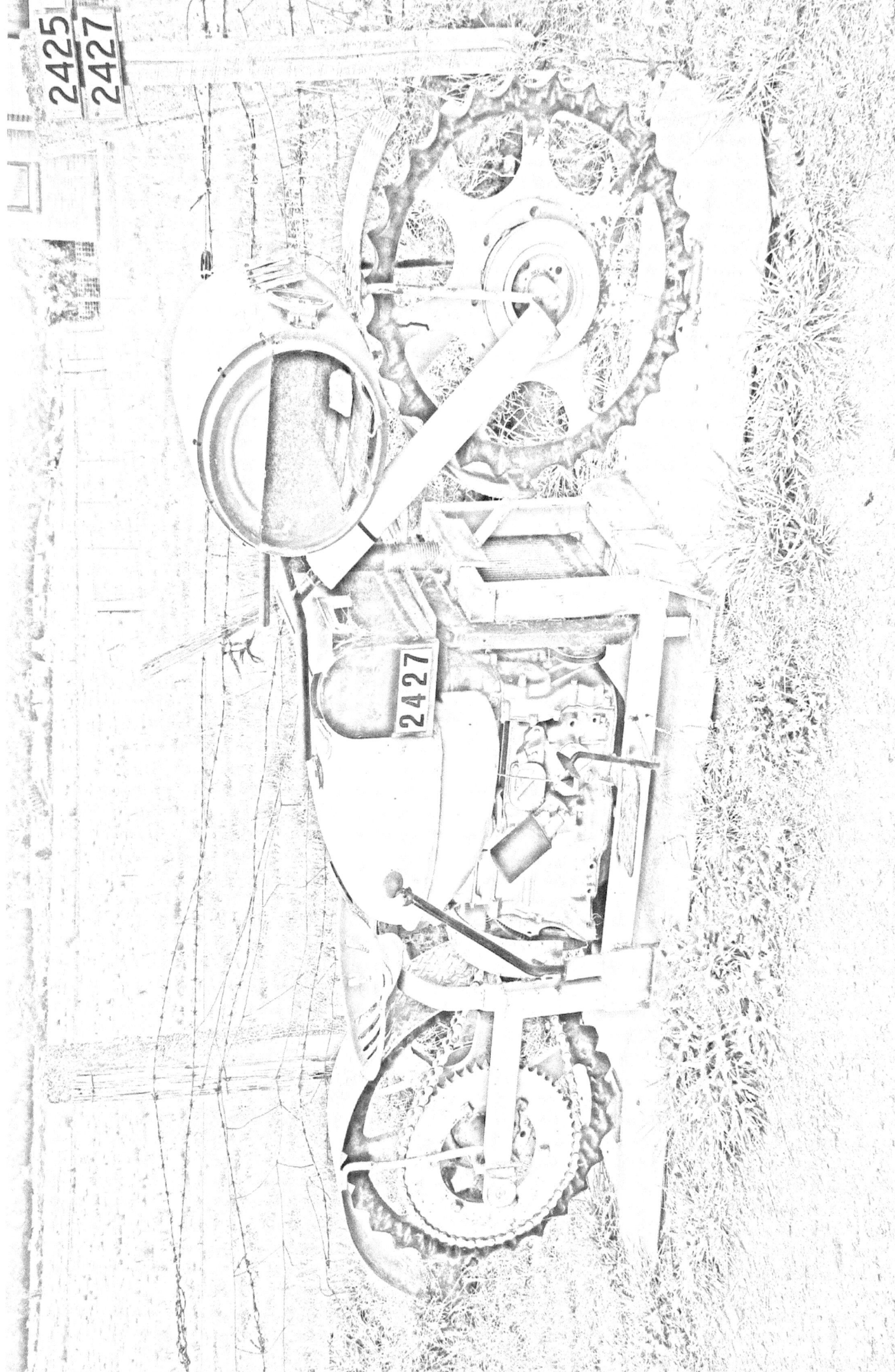

Lighthouse

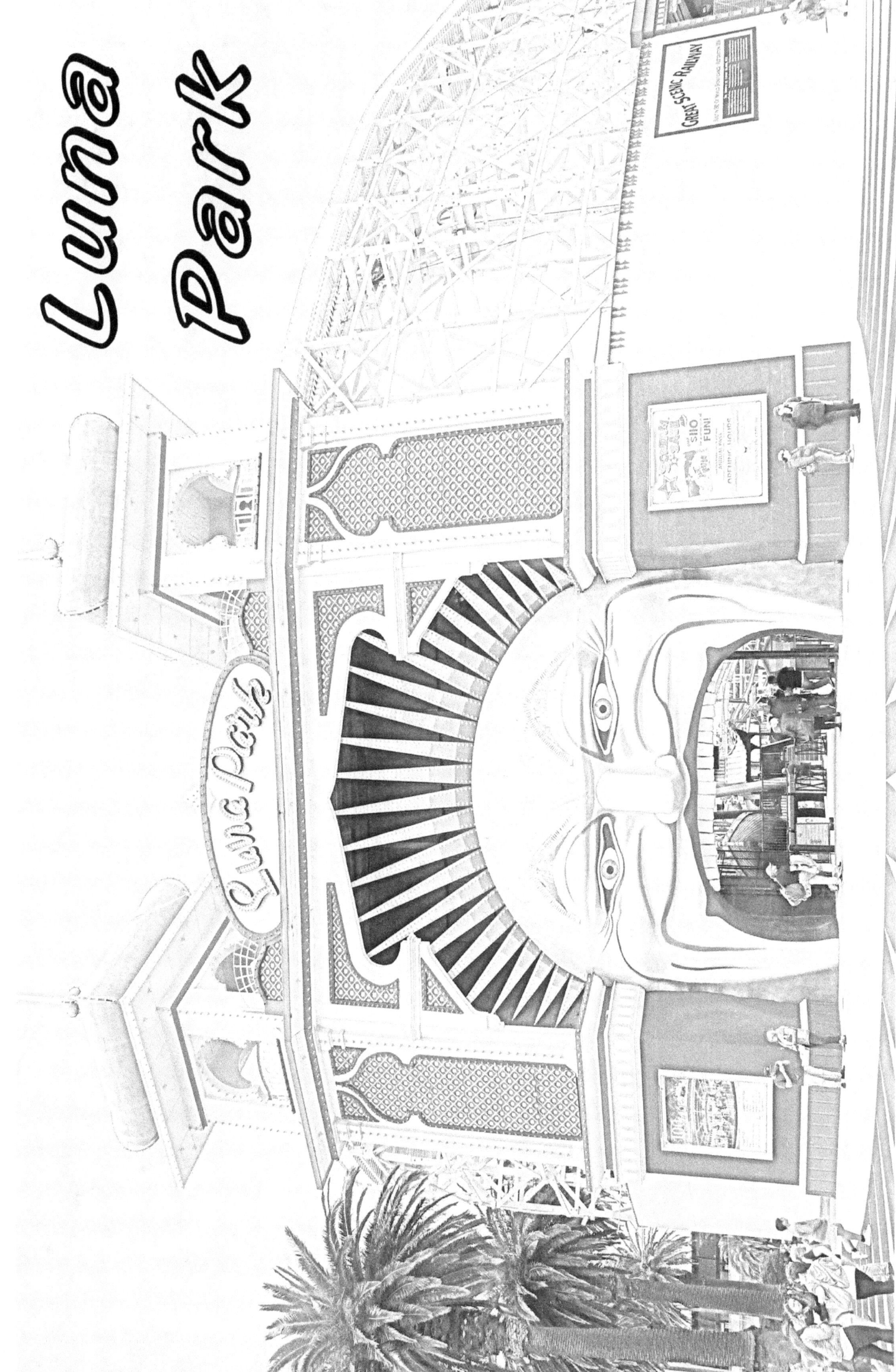

Luna Park

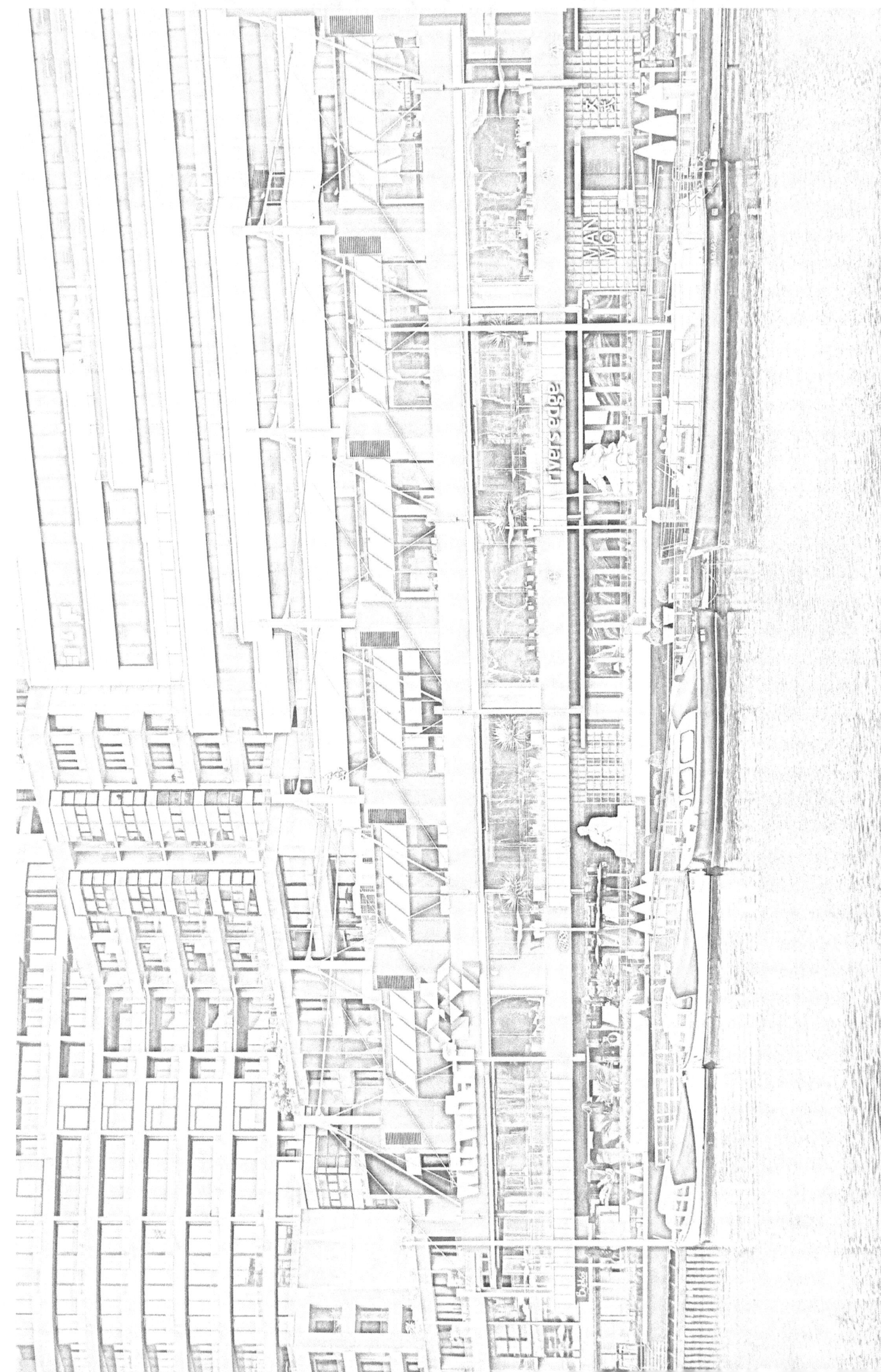

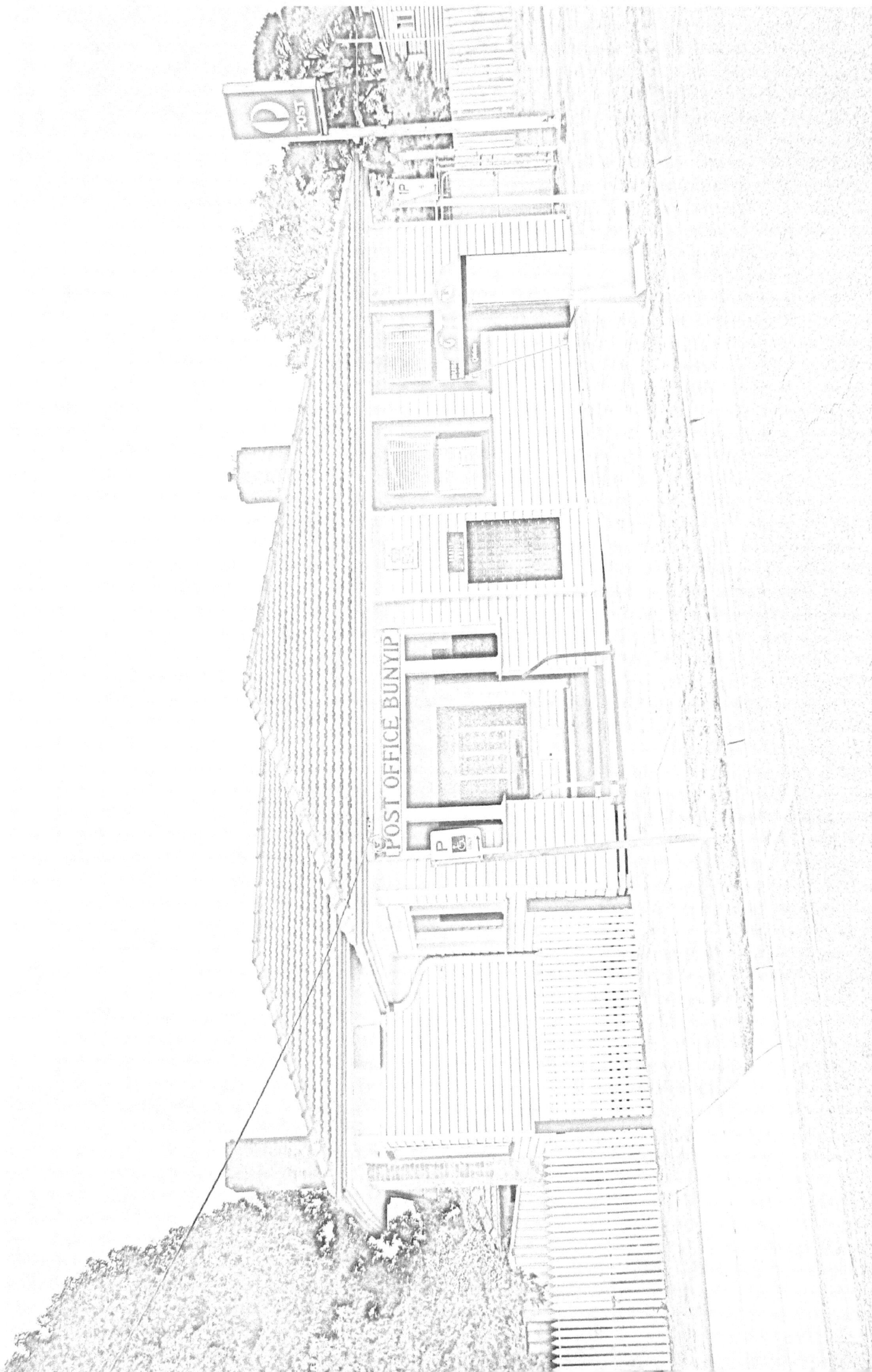

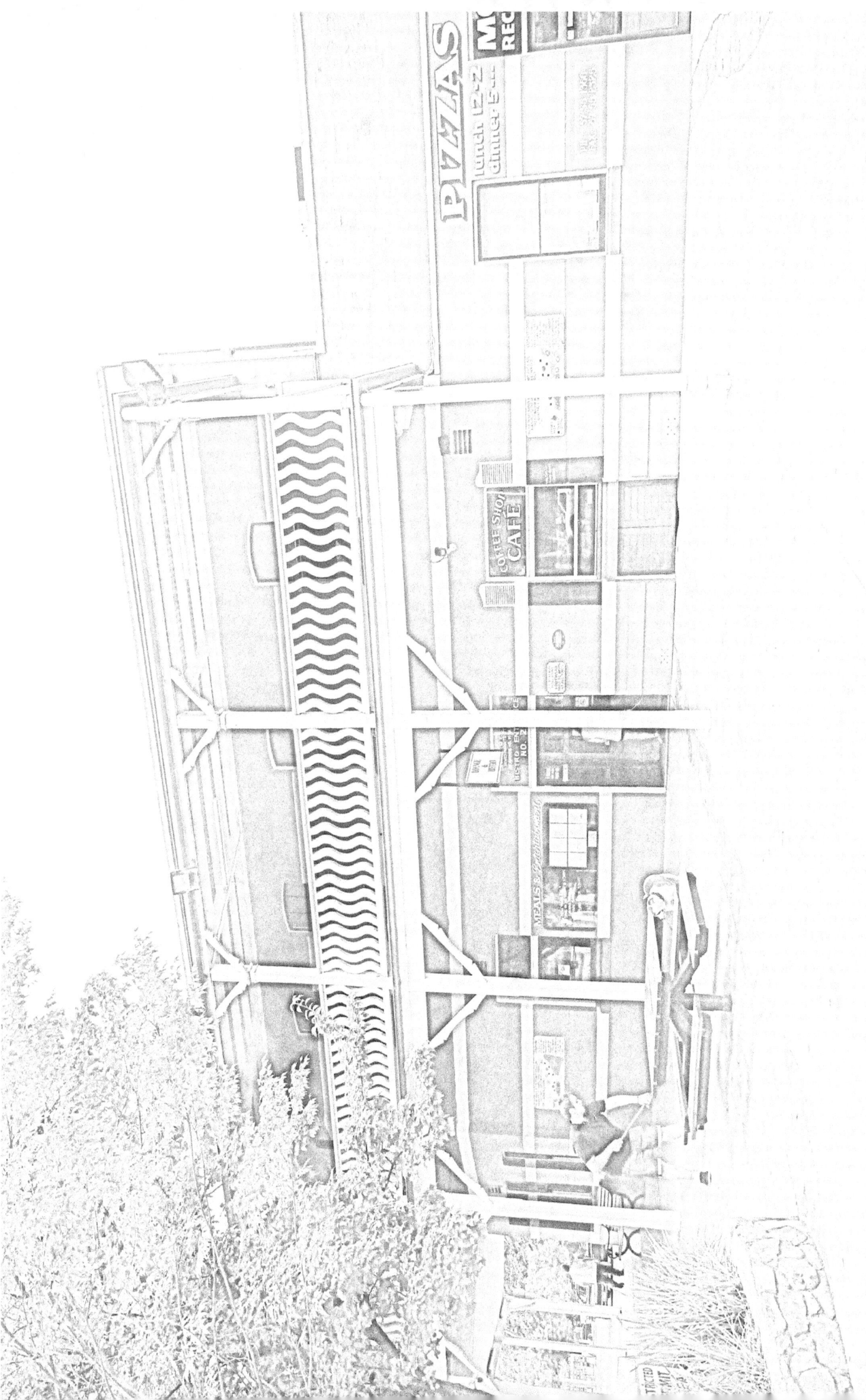

Reptile

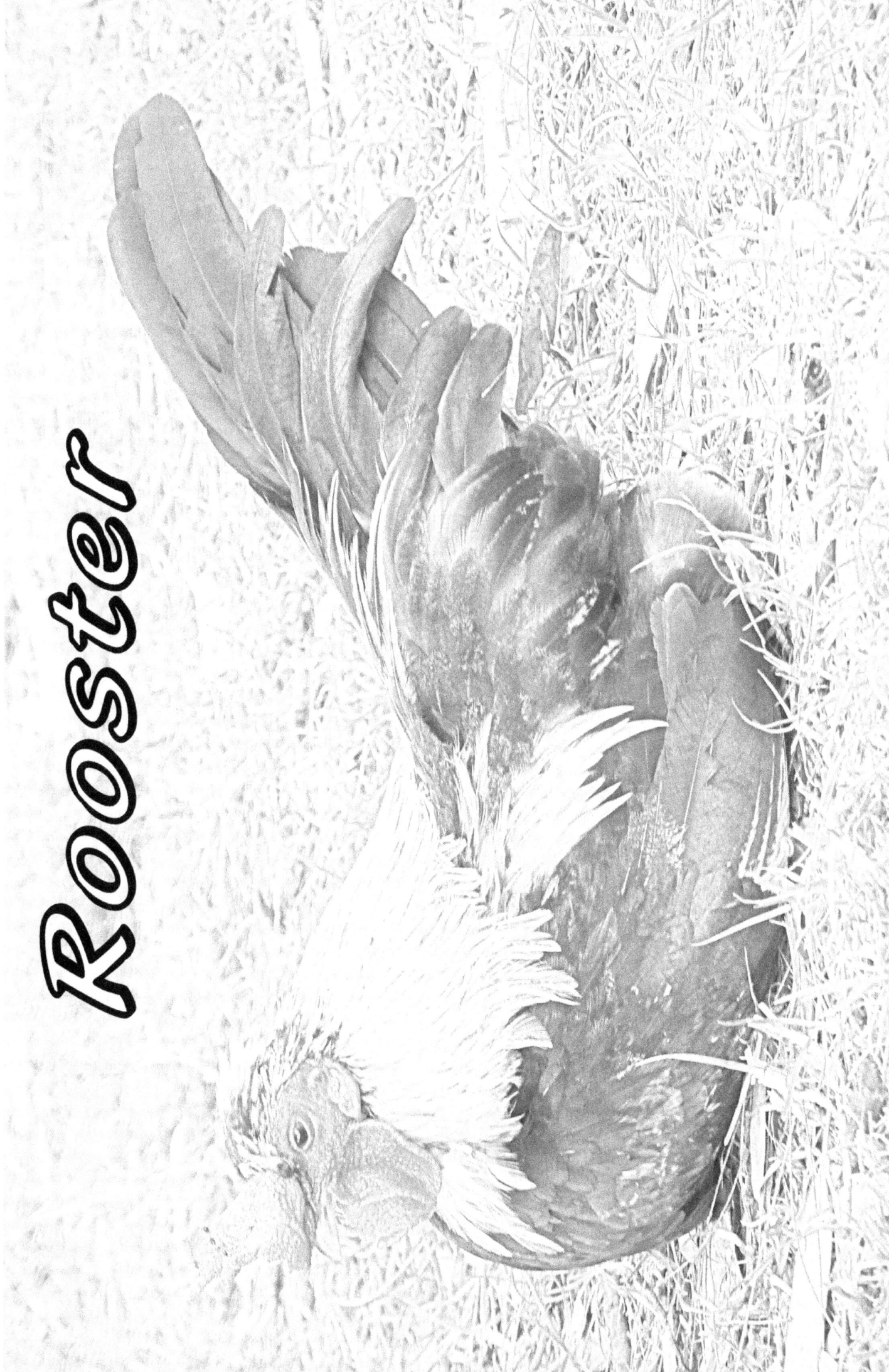

Roooster

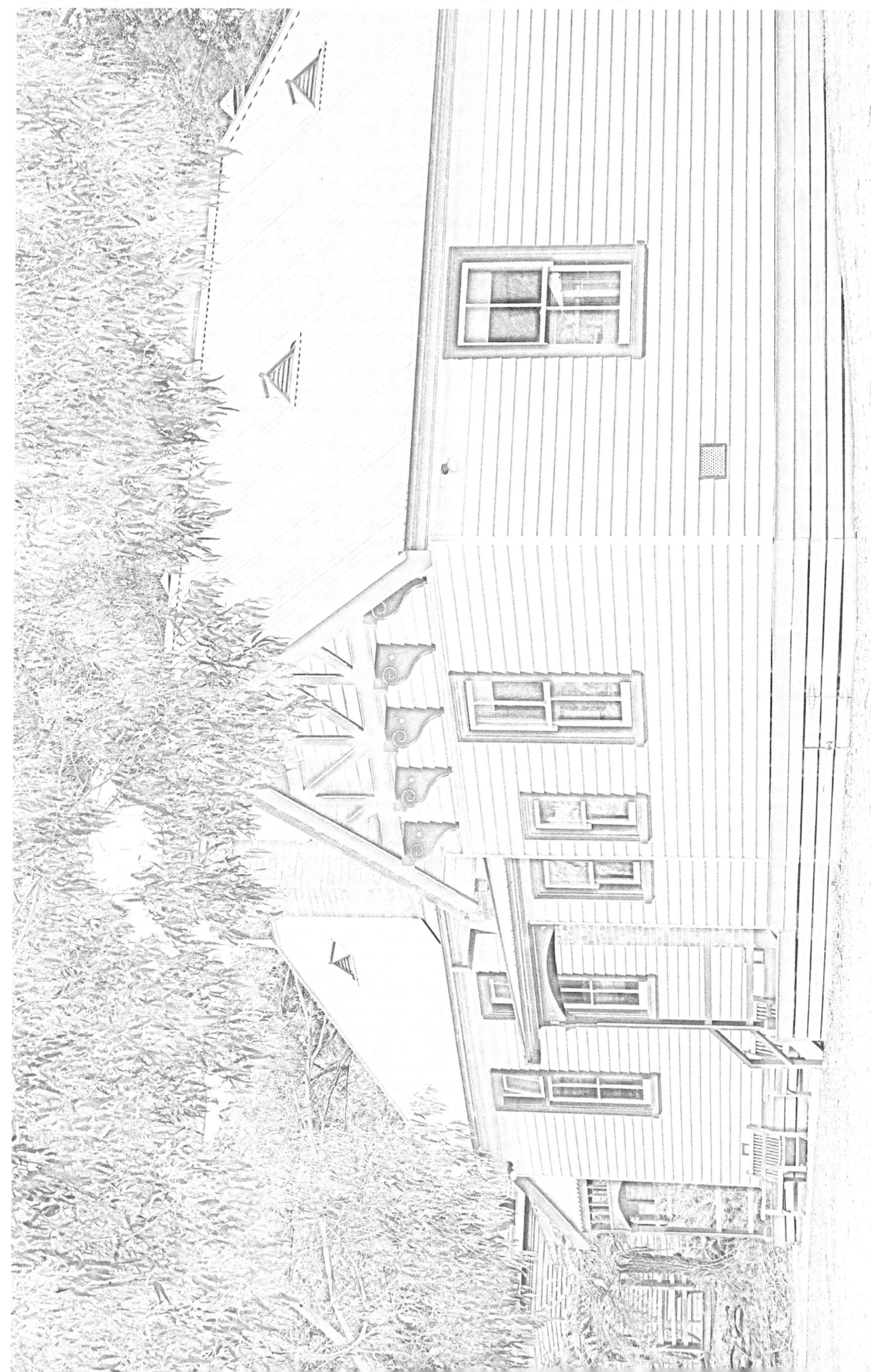

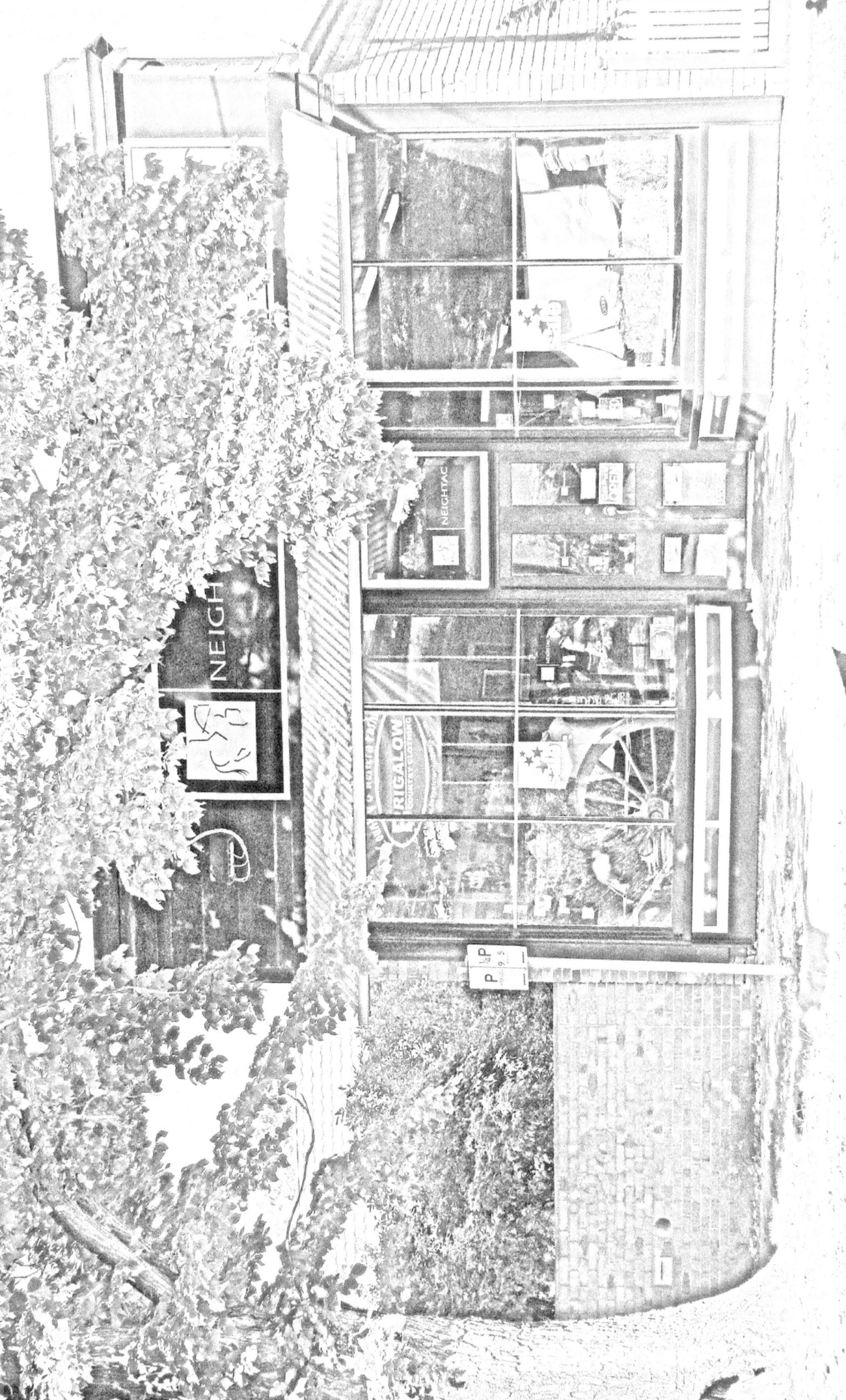

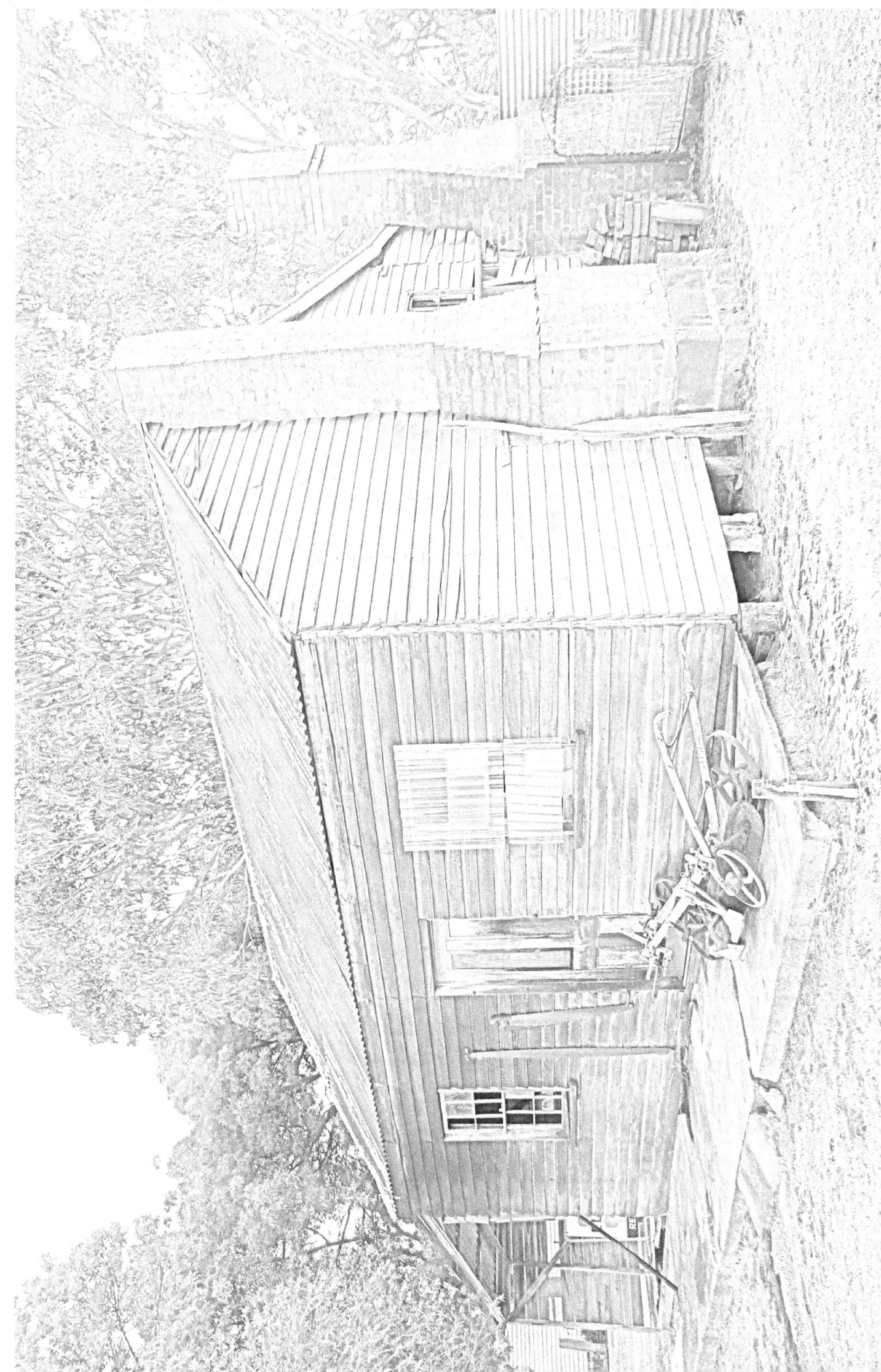

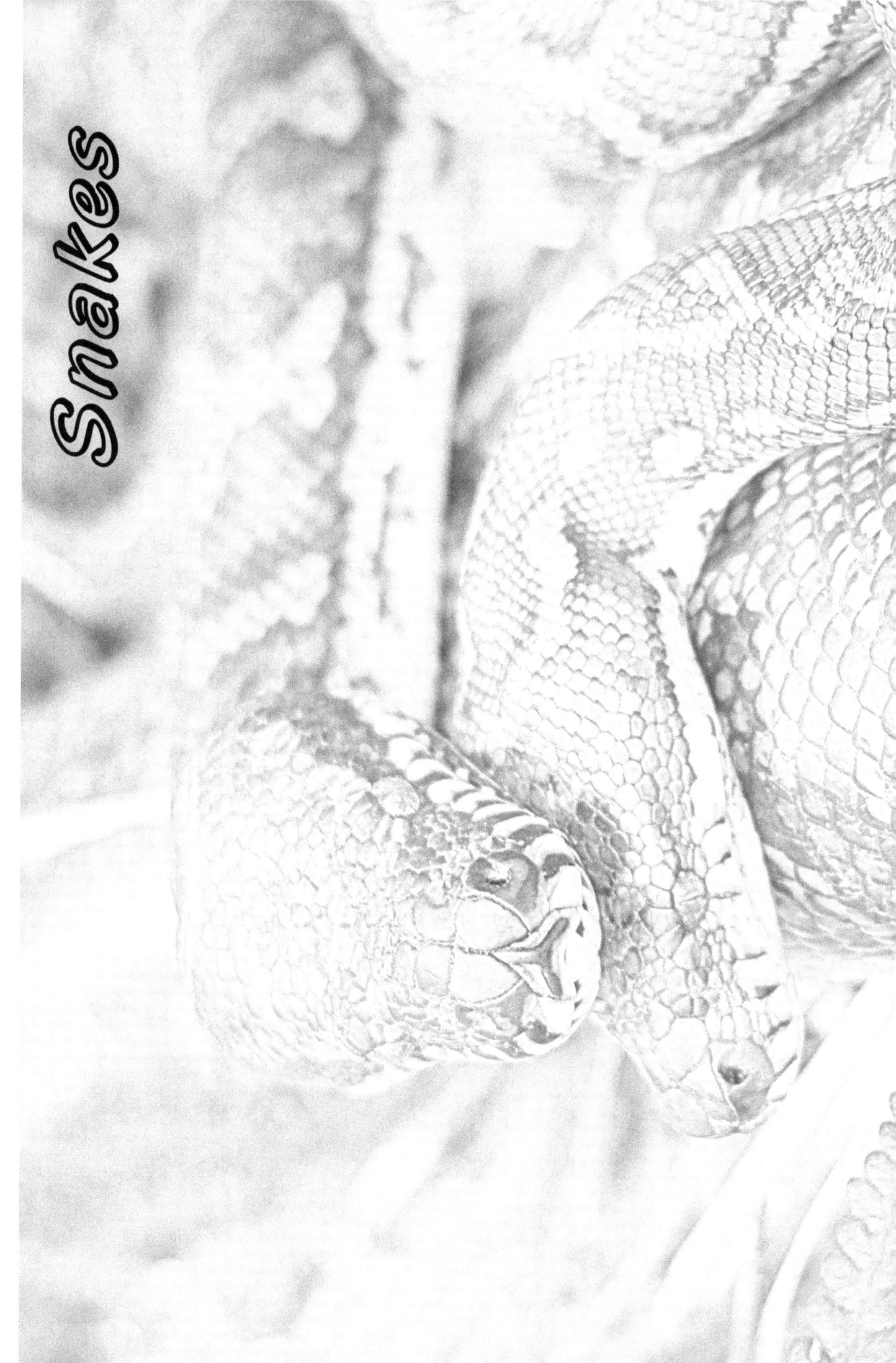

Snakes

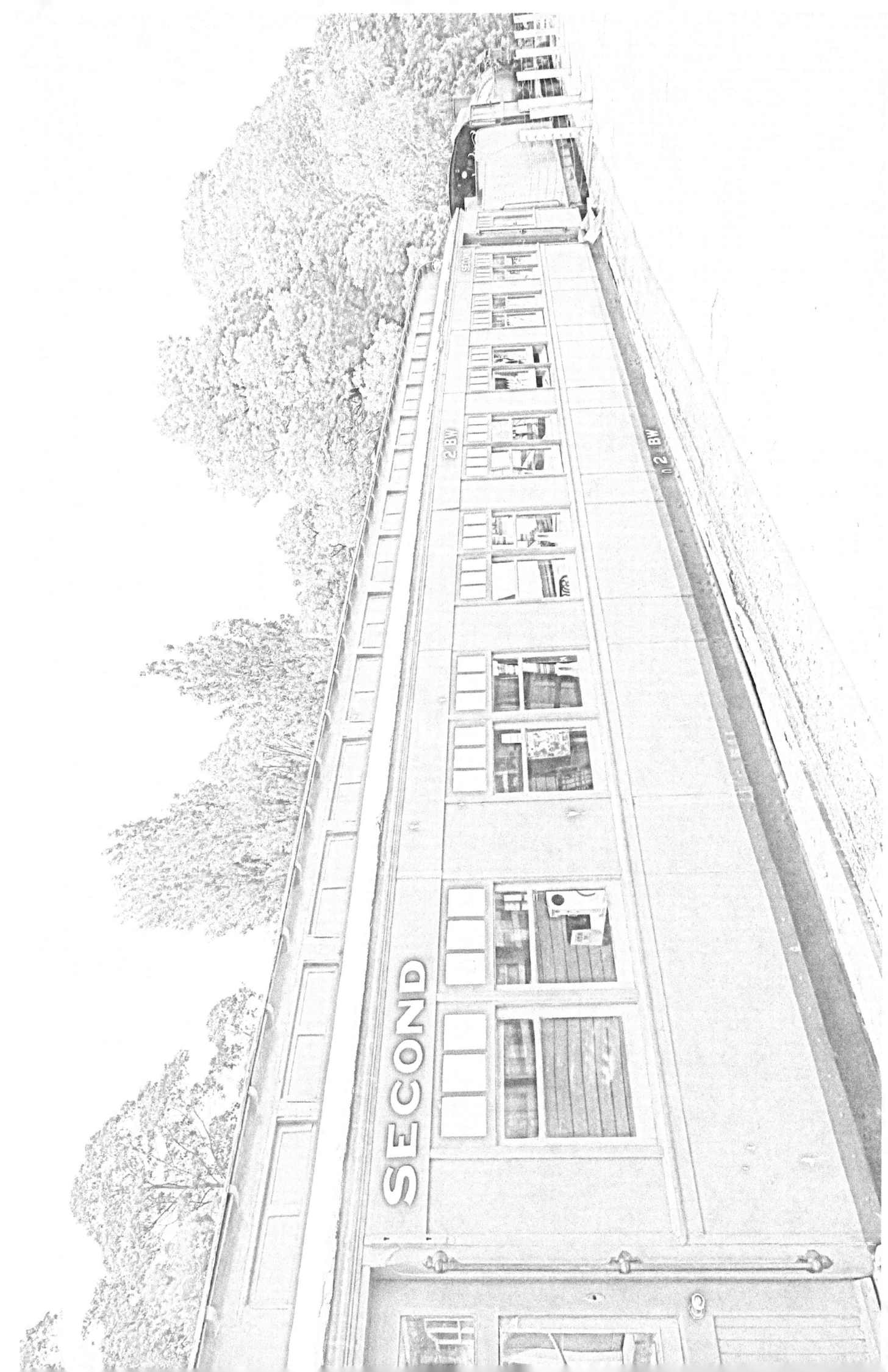

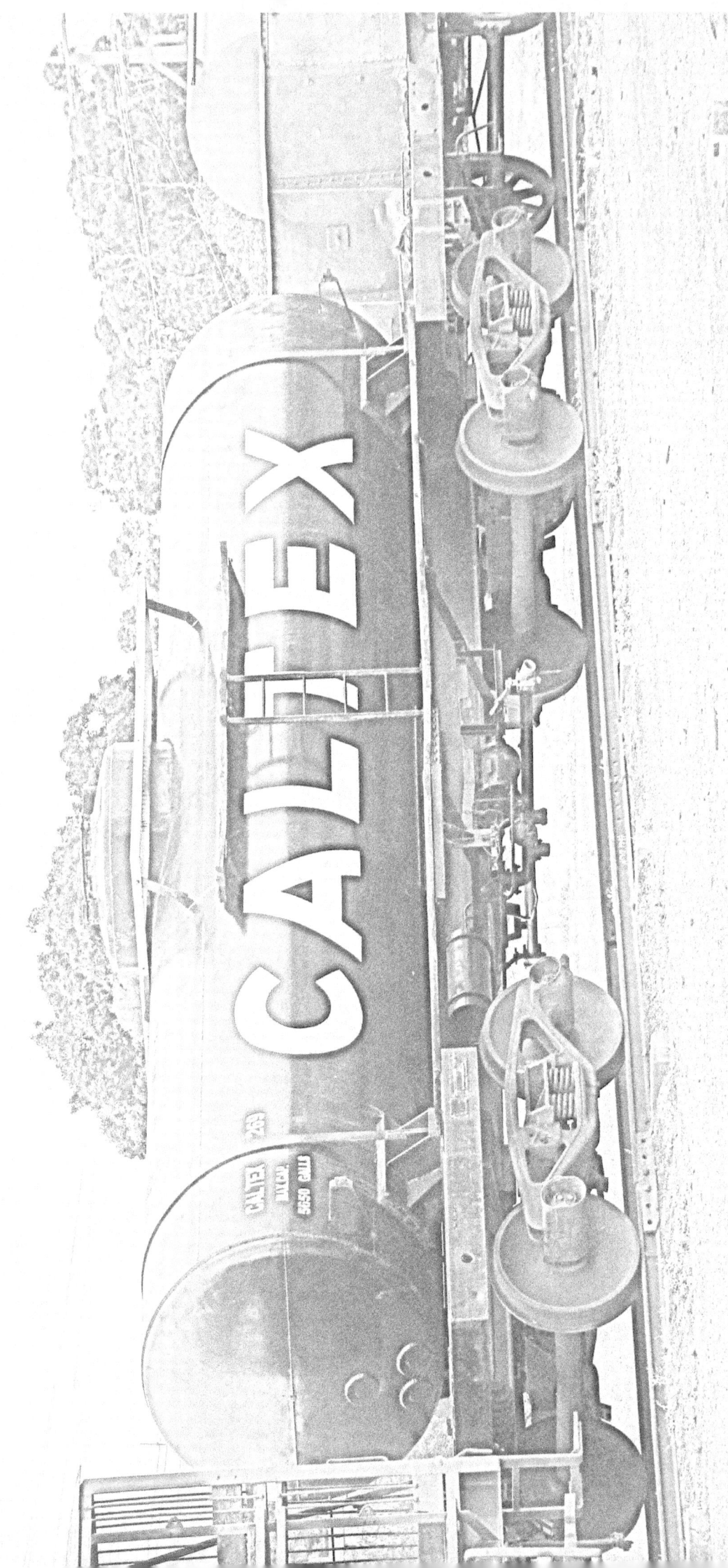

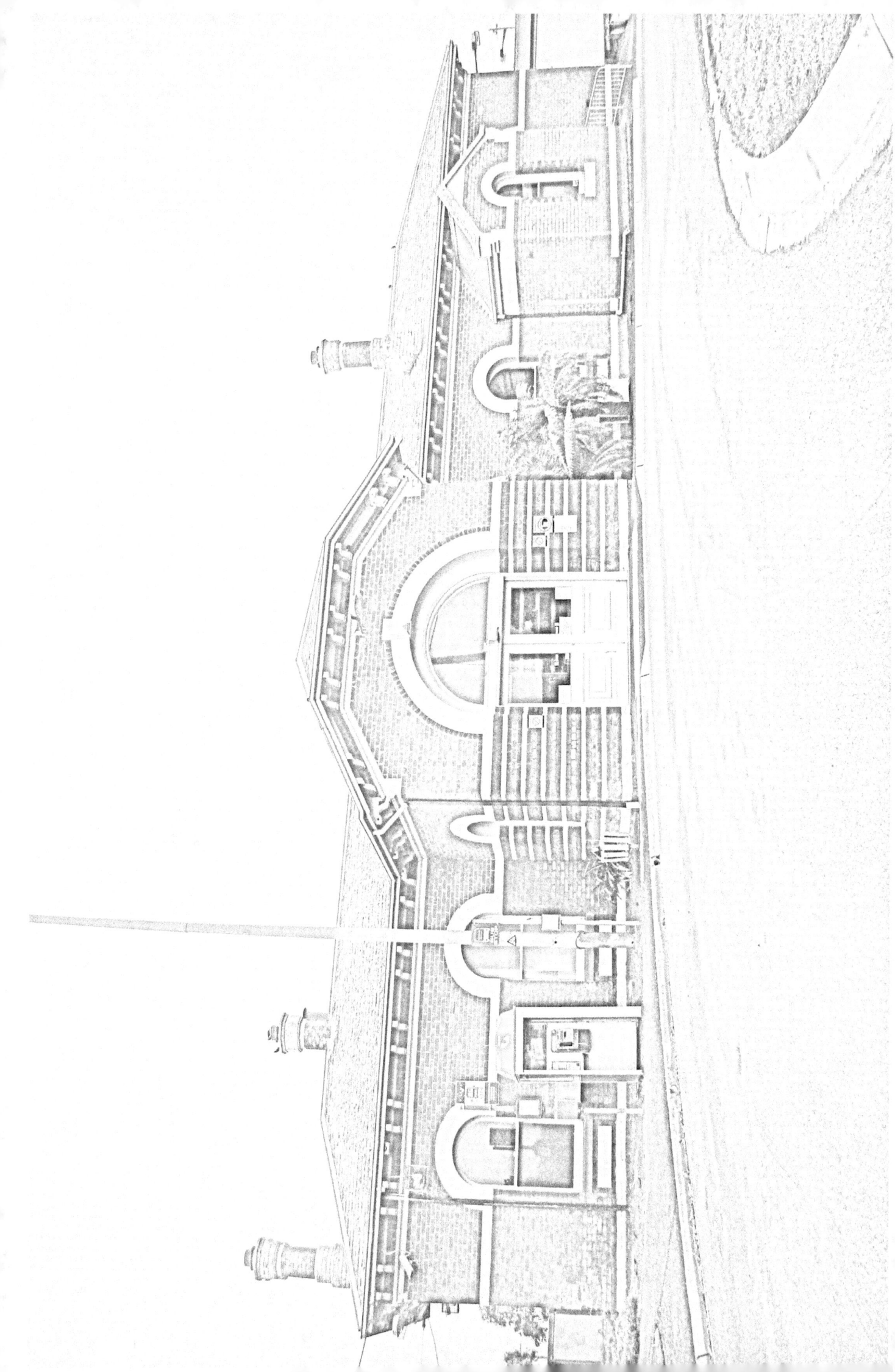

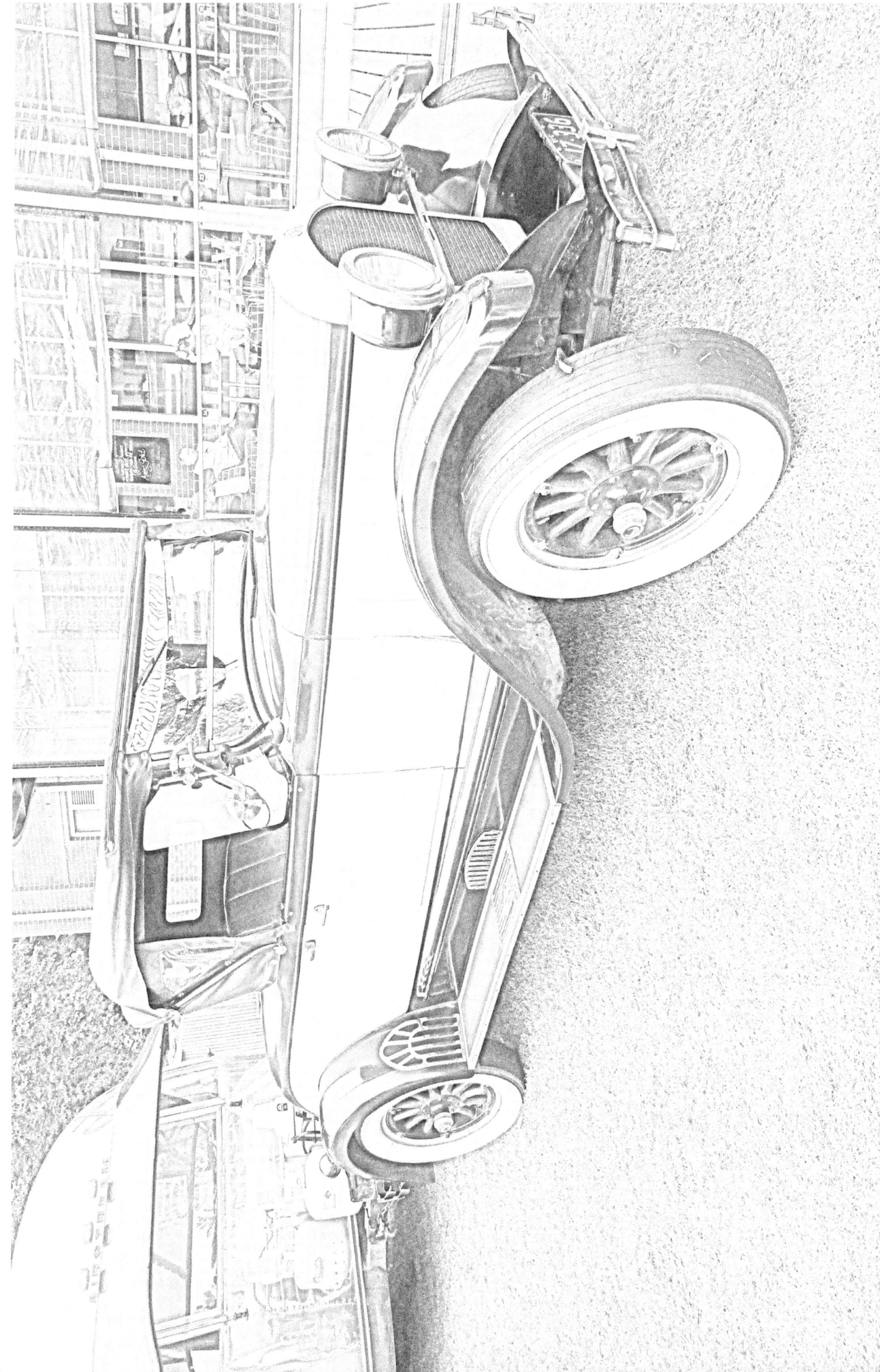

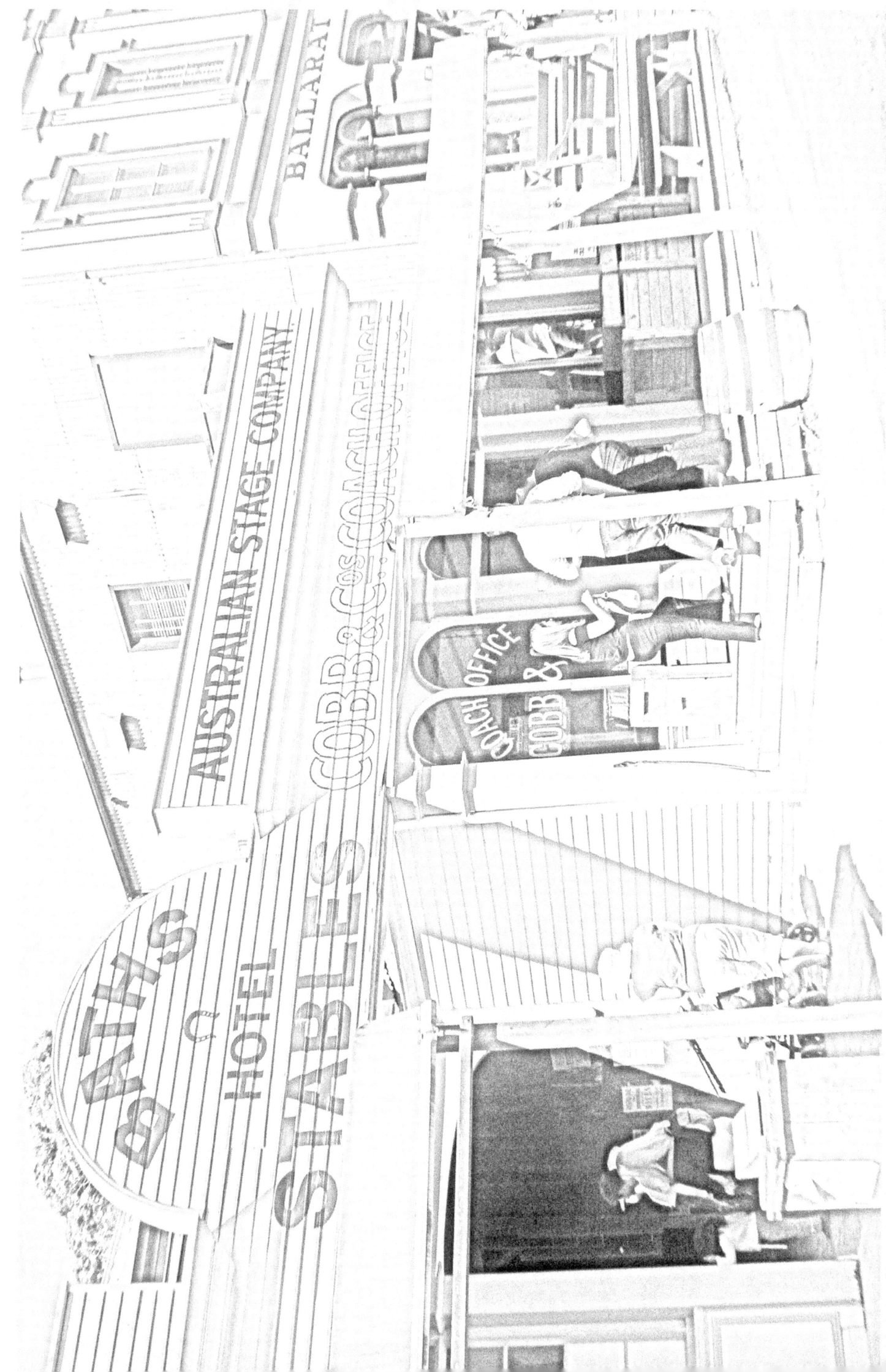

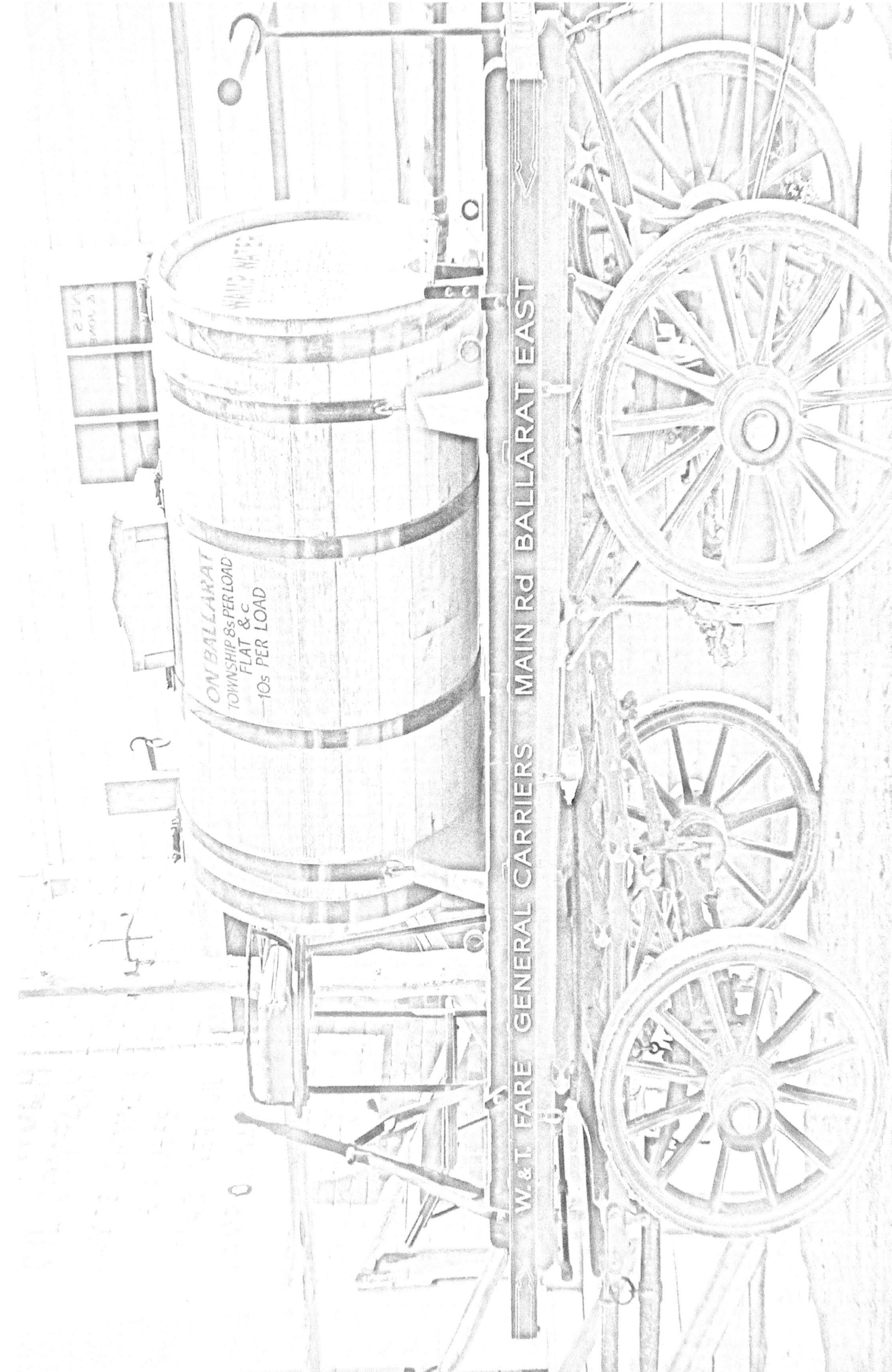

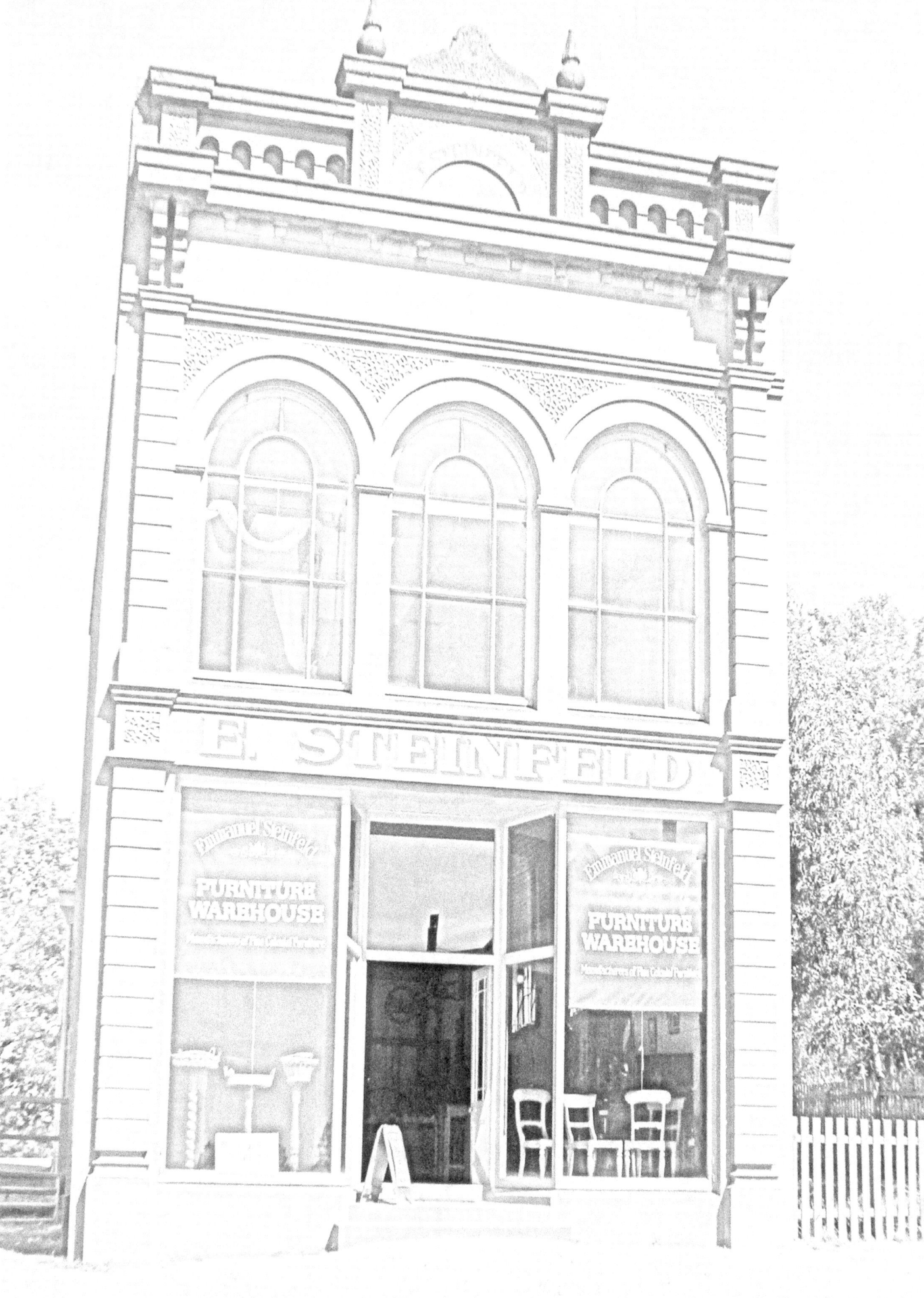

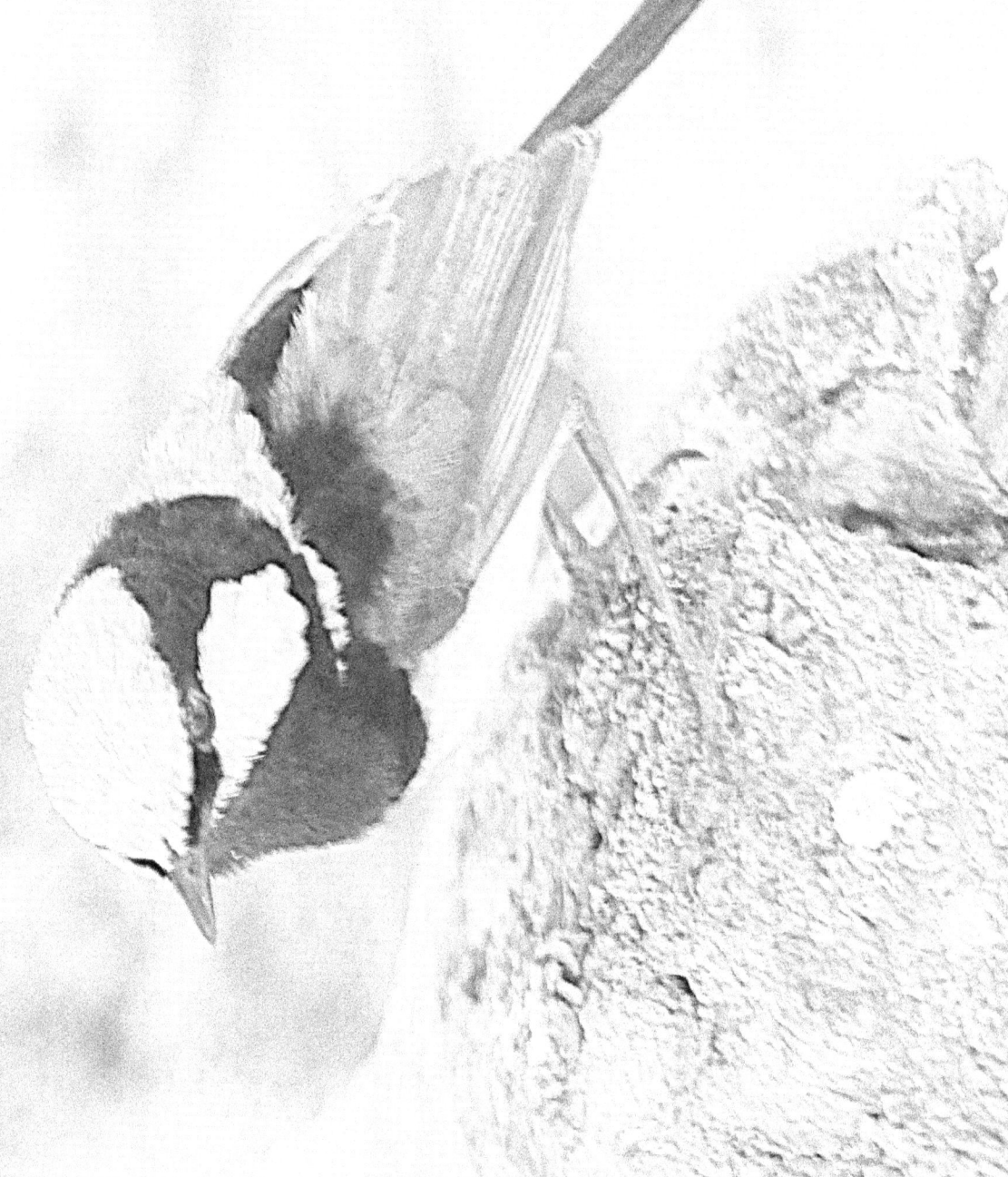

Wren

Big Merino

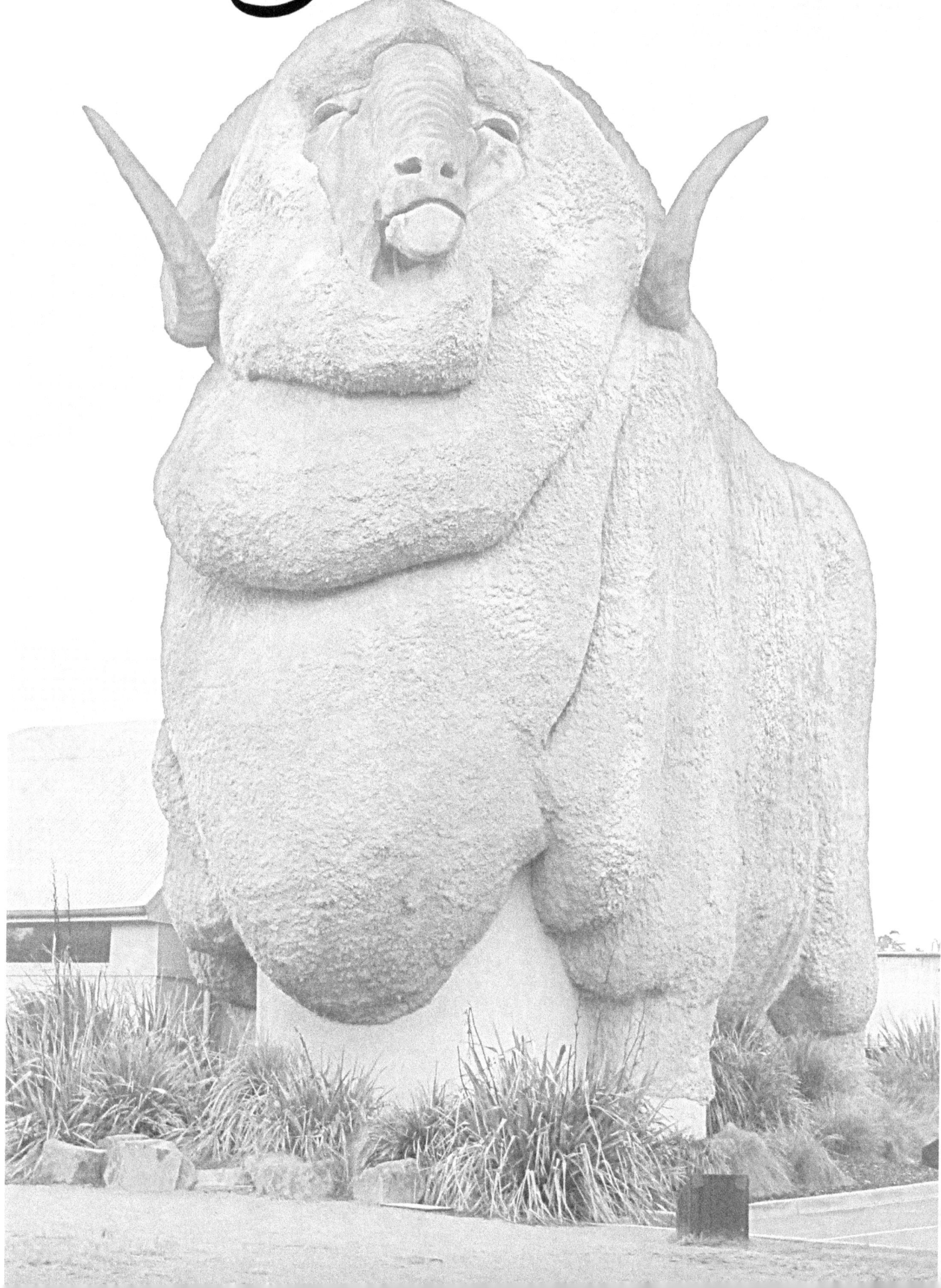

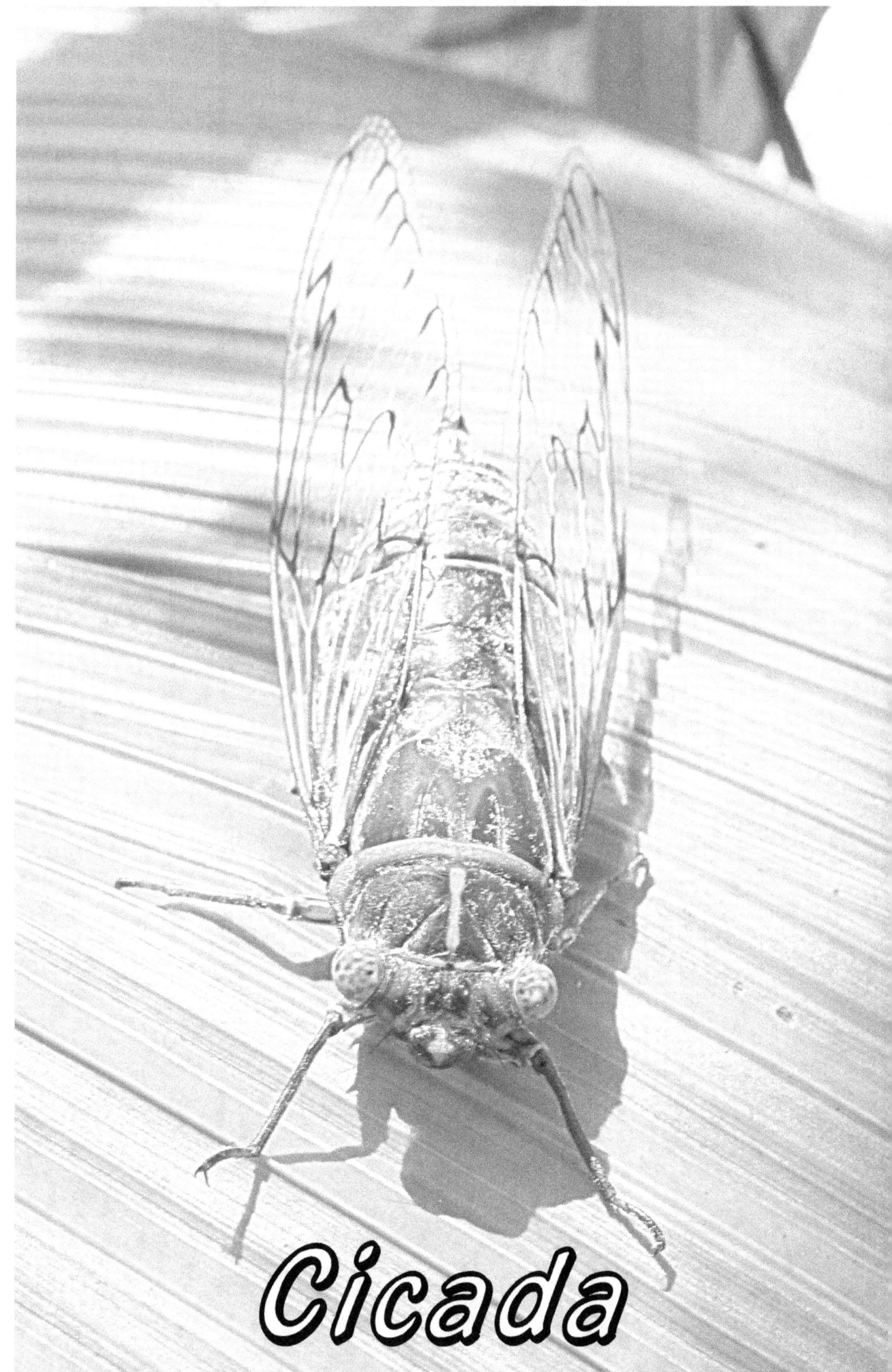

Cicada

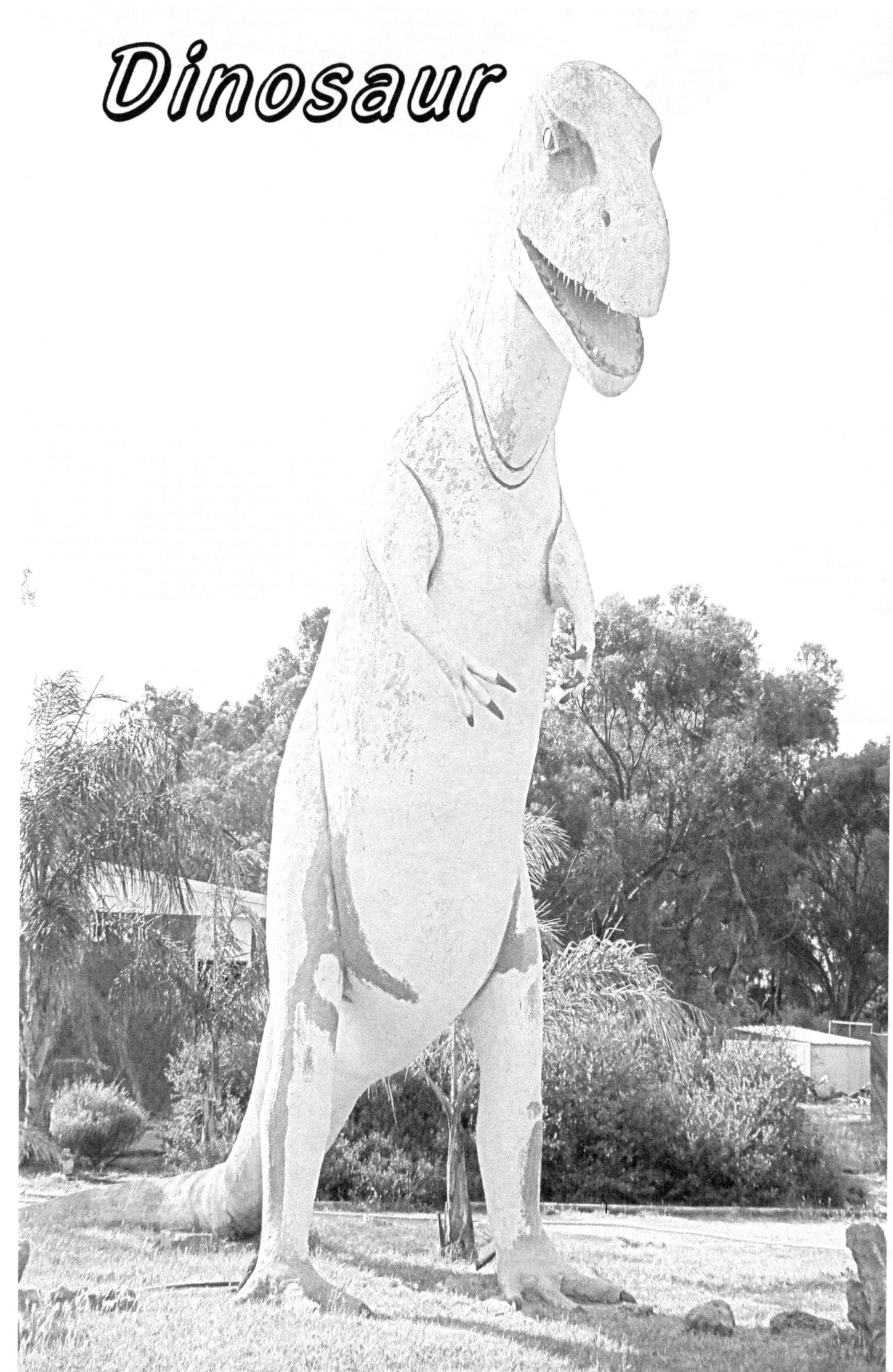

Dinosaur

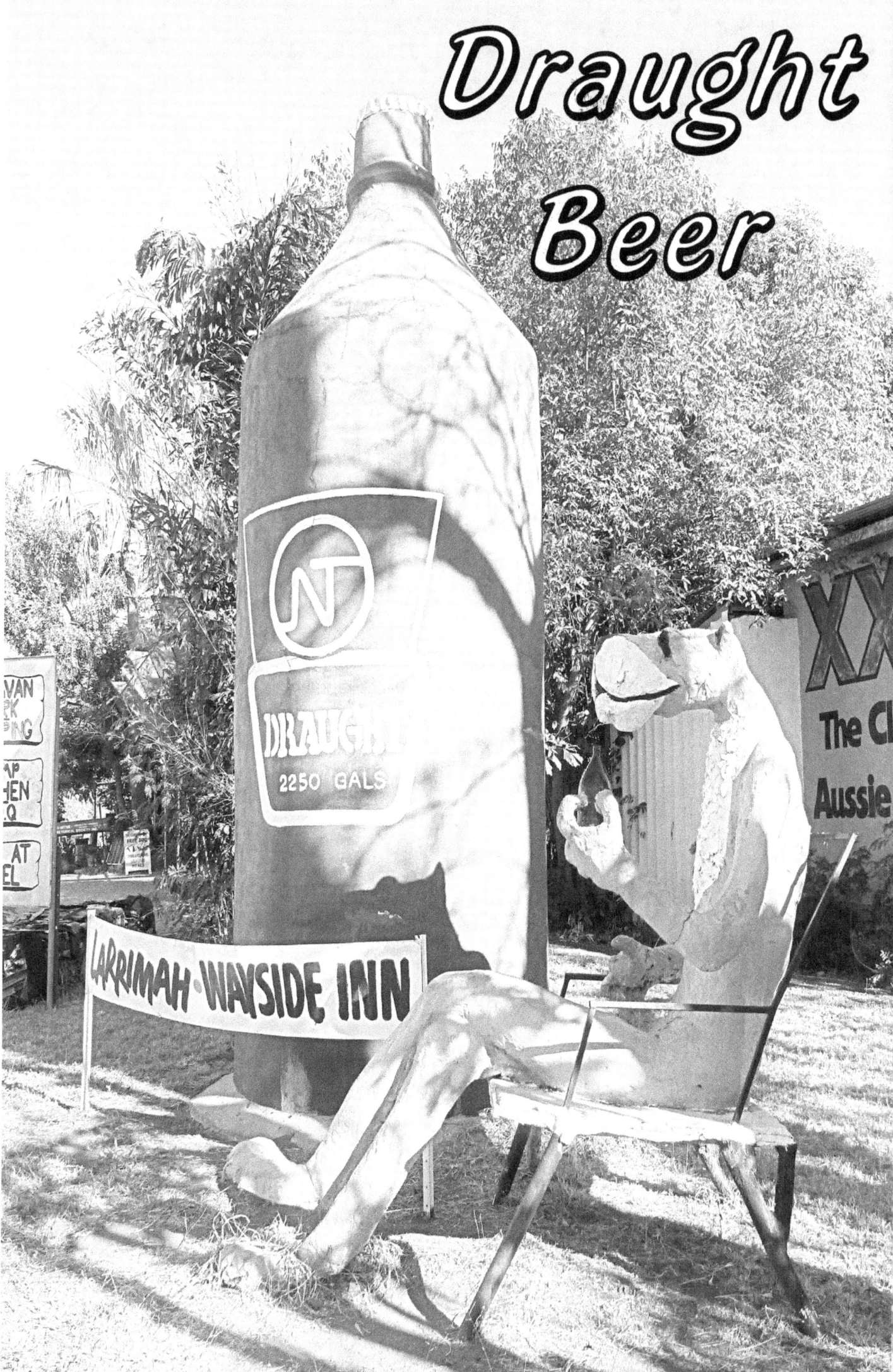

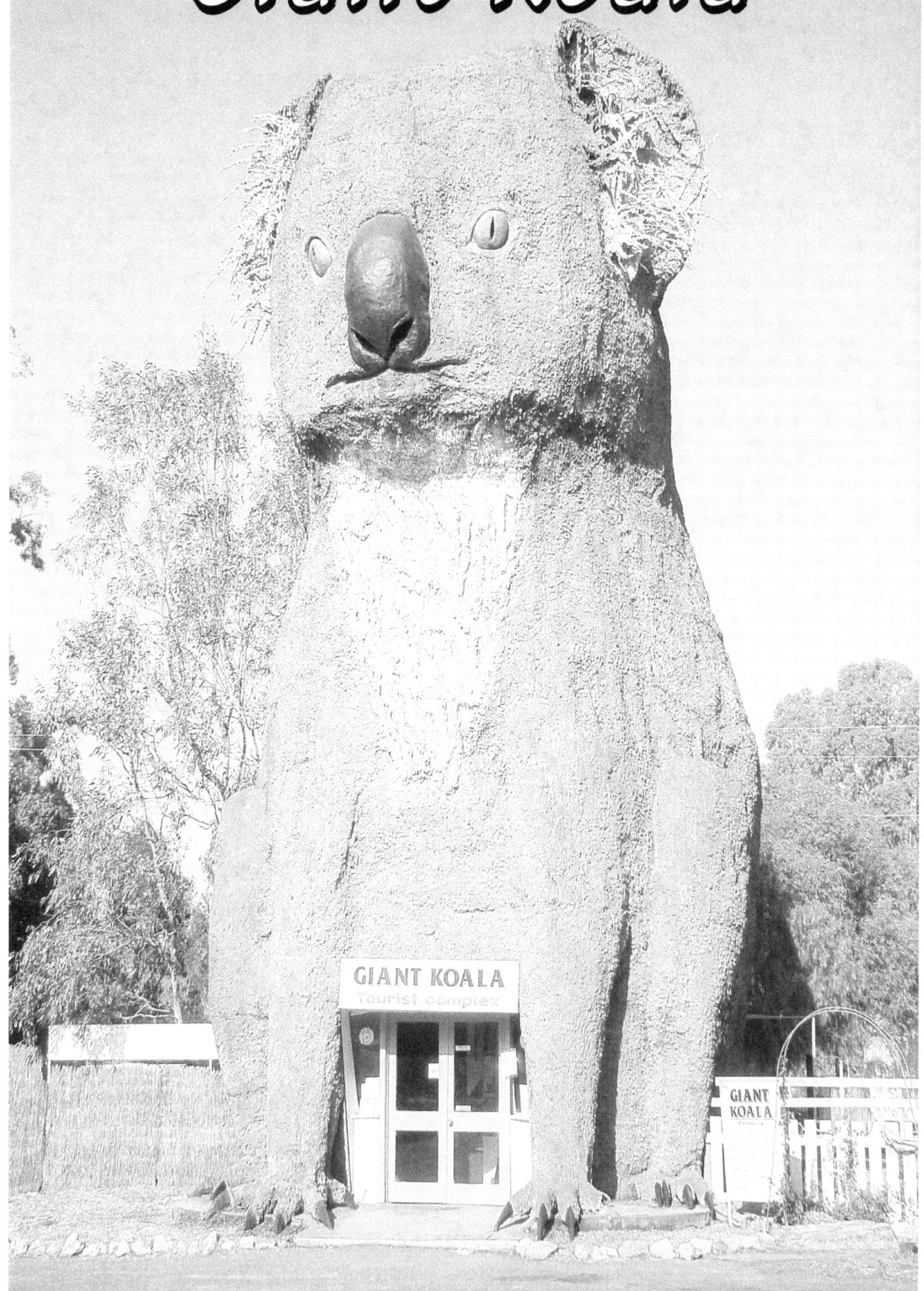

Giant Koala

Lighthouse

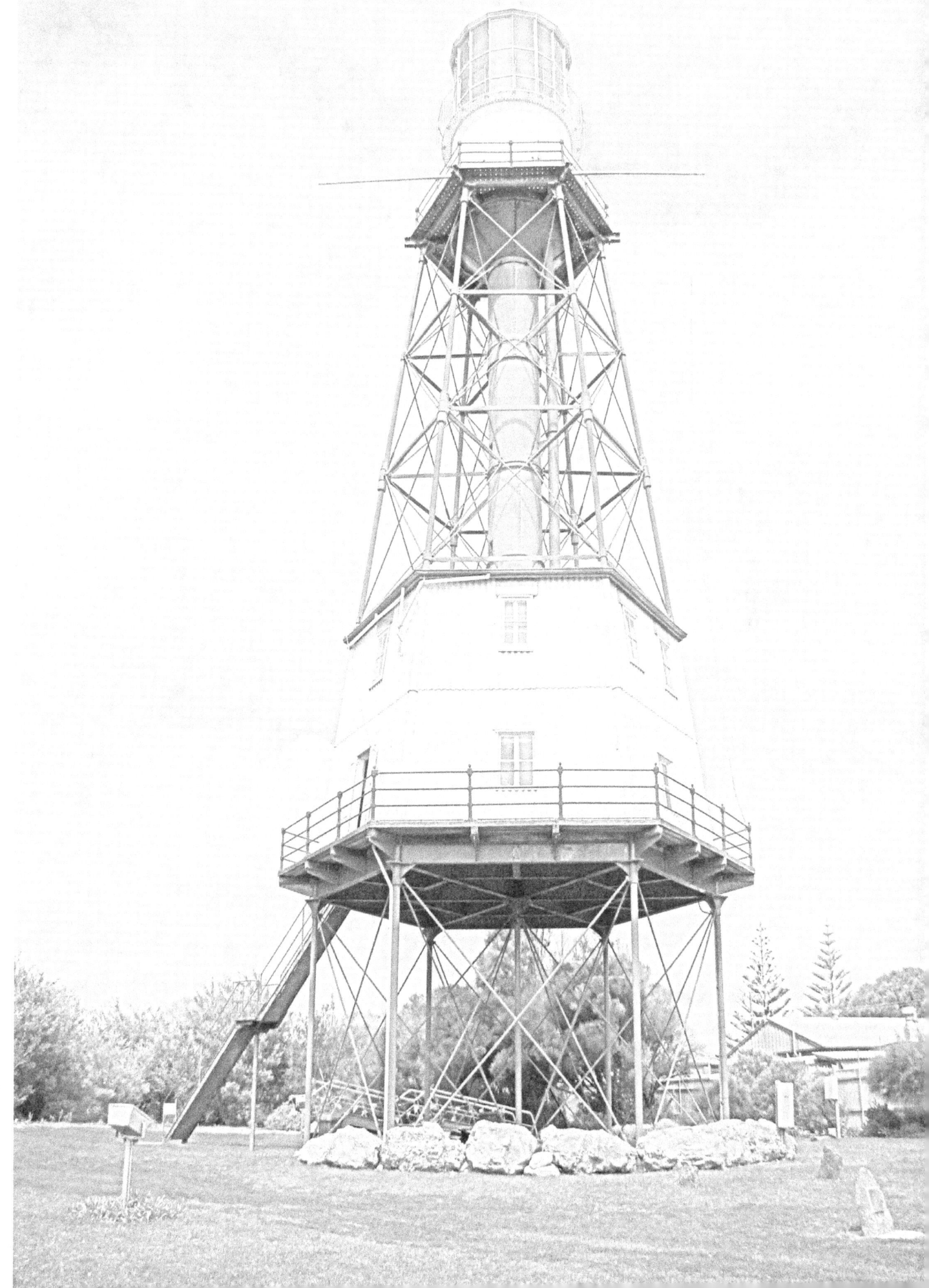

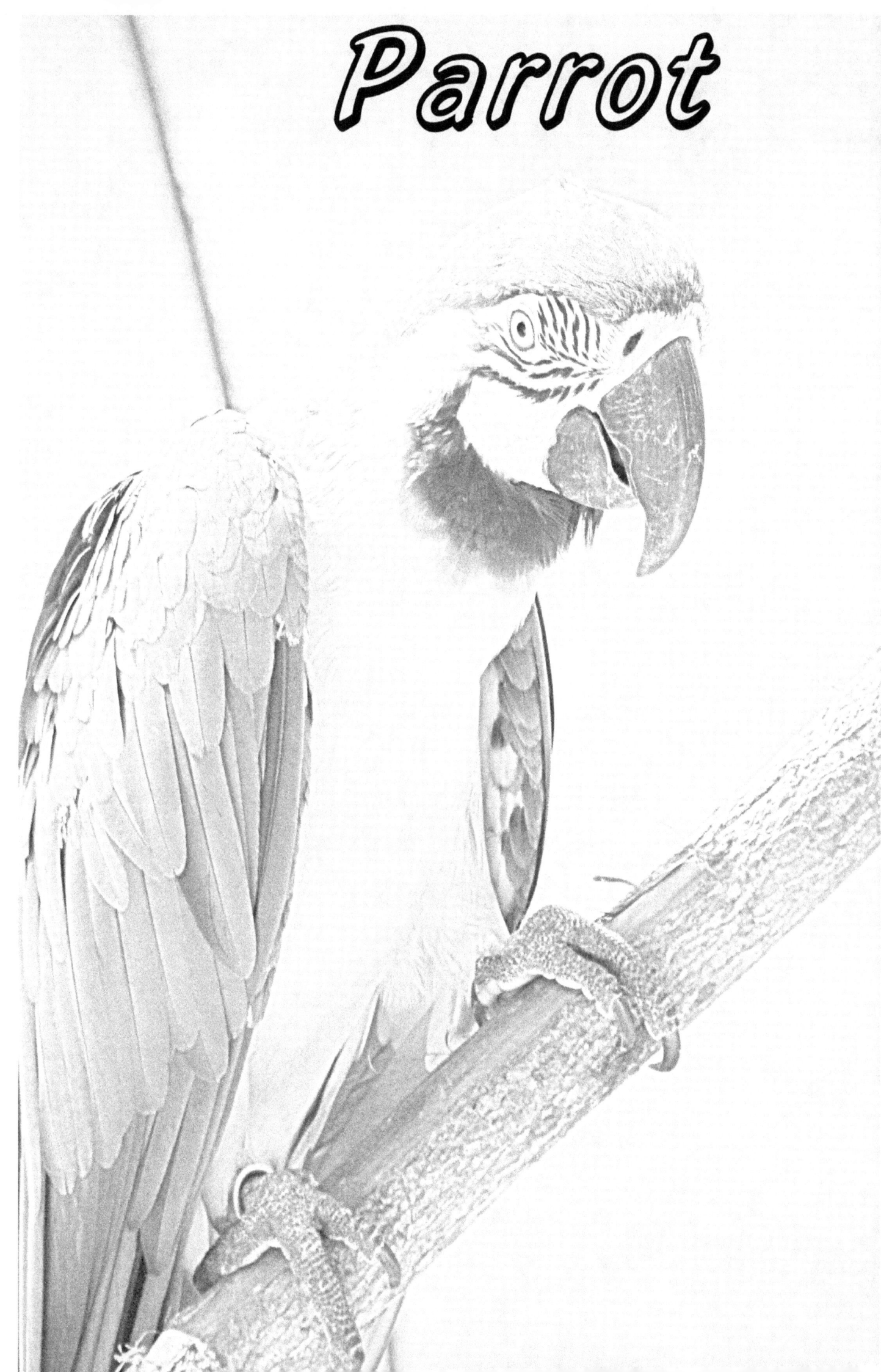

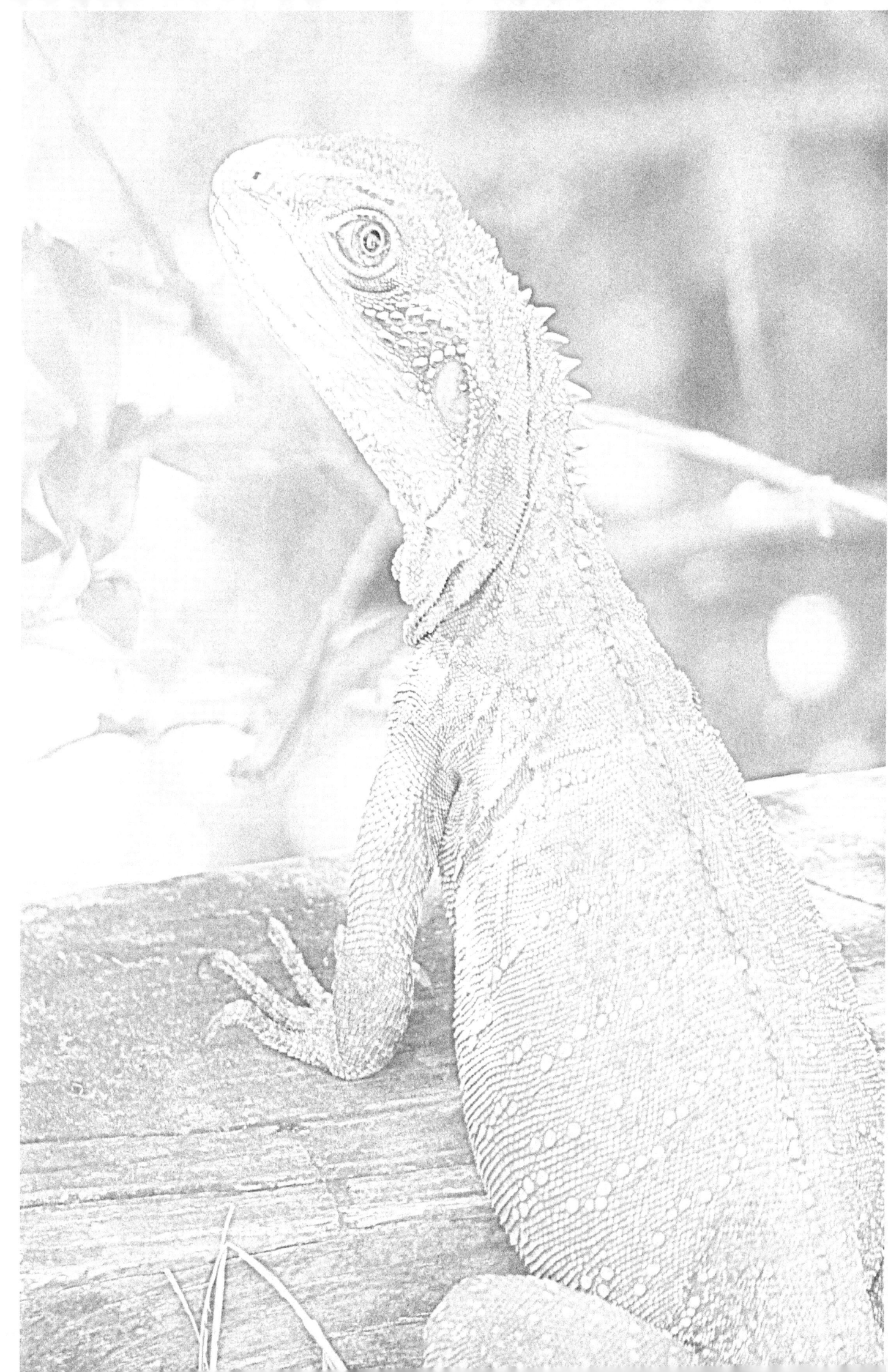

www.ingramcontent.com/pod-product-compliance
Lightning Source LLC
Chambersburg PA
CBHW081048180526
45170CB00005B/1734